MY INCREDIBLE LIFE'S JOURNEY

Yes, You Also Can Make One

DR. MARGARET P. PRICE

My Incredible Life's Journey
Copyright © 2021 by Dr. Margaret P. Price

Tellwell Talent
www.tellwell.ca

ISBN
978-0-2288-6610-7 (Hardcover)
978-0-2288-6609-1 (Paperback)
978-0-2288-6608-4 (eBook)

TABLE OF CONTENTS

ACKNOWLEDGEMENTS

There are many persons without whose suggestions and encouragement the writing of this memoir would not have been started, and others without whose support, guidance, and encouragement it definitely would not have come to conclusion. I thank the Lord for bringing them into my life. The first important person who planted the idea into my head was my now deceased friend for more than forty-five years, May Mills. I met May when I started work as Director of Nursing at London Psychiatric Hospital in Canada, in 1972. She was one of the coordinators and I believe she understood my need for a supportive friend. Over the years, our friendship grew into a sisterhood and she would keep in touch with me and visit me in which ever country I had the opportunity to work. Her last visit to me was just before I left Ghana and we decided to share our future years between Canada and Tobago. Unfortunately, her health began to fail, and that plan could not materialise. However, when I visited her in Canada, she suggested that I should write my memoirs. She said that I had a story to tell that should motivate others, as it had done her.

I was not sure of what I was to write, and I did not really think that anyone would be interested, but I decided to draft an outline. I had originally thought that the book would tell of my professional achievements, but little did I know that the Lord would take control and the book would rather highlight my Spiritual as well as my social and emotional growth as part of my life's journey.

I thank the late Rev. Fr. Marshal Beriault who introduced me to the Cursillo movement in 1965 and put me on the path of Service to my fellowman. As I embarked on the telling of my journey, I shared the first outline with two of my sisters, one younger, Janet Mc Kenzie, and one older, Cynthia Granderson. I trusted them to give me their honest views and to fill in any important details of my childhood that I might otherwise have left out. They were excited and supportive of the idea and added a few of their memories, so I decided to continue.

As the writing continued, I decided that I should contact a few others to get their reactions and inputs. I got feedback from six of my adopted children, as well as two friends, a member of my husband's family and the brother of one of my adopted daughters. These are included in the Chapter on Legacy. Their responses motivated and encouraged me to continue writing.

Finally, there are three most important persons whom I must acknowledge. The first is Ansel Leslie, an adopted nephew who assisted with the typing. The second is another adopted niece, Ms Torie Williams, who provided the drawings for the cover, and last but by no means least is Ms Agnes Murray, who not only provided her editing skills, but also encouraged me to persevere when I frequently felt like giving up.

PROLOGUE

This memoir is written, first to give thanks to God for the many blessings He has bestowed on my life. It is also intended to pay tribute to the many people who contributed to my success: my parents, siblings, early catechists, teachers, priests, good friends, fellow society and group members and workmates, who have touched my life in special ways. It also says a special thank you to all those who supported me with their prayers, love and guidance, and those who served as channels of God's grace, in providing me with opportunities to serve and grow into the happy, largely fulfilled, contented and blessed person that I am today. It recounts my journey, growth and achievements-- intellectually, professionally, socially, emotionally and spiritually. It attempts to document the inter-relationship among these areas of my life.

This autobiography was started because of repeated promptings from others who encouraged me to share my life's story, and affirmation from my inner voice. It is my hope that it would be in some way beneficial to others, particularly some younger ones, and those who may be tempted to limit their dreams by believing that because they are from a small island, a rural, under-developed area, a poor or lower class family, or who fear discrimination in some form. It has been my experience and belief that, even though very difficult at times, listening to, discerning and following what seems to be the will of God, above what I would like to do, brings unimaginable success, contentment, fulfilment, joy, happiness, peace and love. As I write this today, I am still on my Journey. I am in my 85th year, but according to others, I look at least 10 years younger. I attribute this to being happy and stress free, as I have taken seriously the admonition to cast my burdens on the Lord.

I have worked hard and always endeavoured to give of my best. I have been privileged to live, work, develop and use my skills in more than two dozen countries, as well as visit and socialize in nineteen others, practically spanning the globe. I know that I did not do this on my own. In addition to continuously striving to grow educationally, I had to grow spiritually, socially and emotionally along the way. This enabled me to withstand and survive the challenges that came my way, and to emerge a happy and satisfied person. I will, therefore, be recounting important aspects of these challenges as they inter-relate.

I believe that my young readers can achieve more than I did, while having fun doing so. YES YOU CAN. My journey was not always easy. I went off course a number of times. I sincerely hope, however, that this recounting will be an inspiration for those who choose to read it.

I

THE JOURNEY BEGINS: 1936-1954, Trinidad and Tobago.

1: THE FOUNDATION

1.1: My Parents.

I am of very humble origins, the sixth of eight children of my parents, Benjamin and Nora Price.

My father, born in 1889, was also one of a family of eight children. He was educated to the primary level and started his work life as a labourer. However, because of his ingenuity and hard work, he became a landowner, owning properties which he was able to bequeath to each of his children and his first set of grandchildren. He was wise, loving, and understanding. He loved the Lord and believed in service to his family, church, and community. His name is encrypted on one of four cornerstones of the Methodist church in the village of Mason Hall, as attestation to the contributions that he made.

My father did not hesitate to quote the Bible to us. Even though some of his quotations were erroneous, they served his purpose. One such quotation which is imprinted on my psyche, was generally said when we asked for new church clothes for special seasons such as Easter or Christmas. His serious response was, "The bible says, render your heart and not your garments." Not until I grew up and started reading the bible myself, did I realize that God in speaking to the Israelites in Joel 2:13 told them to "rend" their hearts and not their garments. Surprisingly, however, to this day I still believe that in terms of preparing for going to church, I should render my heart, and not worry about what to wear, as long as it is clean and presentable.

My father valued education. Even though he did not obtain much of it, he would describe himself as having "common sense" and insist that he was "no man's fool." He often said that "common sense" was better than "book sense." He was a good provider, loved dancing, and taught us, his daughters, how to dance. We loved that, and I still love dancing. As we grew older, he would take us to afternoon dances in the village on Boxing Day, New Year's Day, and Easter Monday. He enjoyed being the umpire at cricket matches and would take us to watch cricket matches in the village. I remember his love of going to the races, going to other villages at "harvest time" and entertaining others when it was our village's time to do the hosting. He was a smart dresser, was said to like the ladies and based on that was given the nickname, "Sugar Ben."

My father was a strict disciplinarian and my mother used that awareness to keep us in line. If we were doing something wrong and not listening to her, all she had to say was, "Wait 'til your father comes home," and we would give in. We certainly did not want a strapping (any licks). Corporal punishment was acceptable in those days, and again my father would quote the bible to us. He believed that he should not, "Spare the rod and spoil the child." He was no saint, but he made sure that we were adequately provided for and given proper guidance.

My Parents: Benjamin and Nora Price

My mother was 13 years younger than my father. She was born in 1902, and was jet black in complexion. My father described her as a "black beauty." He told us that the first time he saw her he said, "I must marry that black beauty." Her mother was a descendant of slaves, but her father had arrived directly from the Gold Coast (now Ghana) as a seaman with the Merchant Marines. He was from the Ga tribe and his family was among the group of chiefs. His name was Obli Quarcoo, and when he arrived in Tobago, the Ga population there referred to him as Nii Obli. He told my mother about his family and she was able to pass this information on to some of her grandchildren. This enabled me to locate his tribe and family in Ghana, and to have a true sense of belonging during the twenty plus years in which I lived there.

Mamie, my mother, converted from being a Methodist to Catholicism in her youth. To me, she was almost saintly. My father presented her with two other children, and she accepted them as her own. She seemed to have benefited much from the education available to her. She became a "Pupil Teacher," but, unfortunately, as was common in her day, she had to give that up when she got married. She was a devoted wife and mother and seemed to be able to cope with any stress. She was very interested in the education of her children and worked hard, buying and selling things, to ensure that her children received an education, according to our abilities.

My mother was always there for us, ensuring that we were properly nourished, clothed, and well "brought up." She knew how much we looked forward to her presence when we arrived home from school and was almost always there. Most importantly, she made sure that we started off each day with prayer. Every morning, she would wake us up at 5.00 a.m. to pray the Rosary. My father made sure that we were there kneeling at the foot of their bed. Even though he did not participate in the praying of the Rosary, he imparted what knowledge he had about the importance of love of God, family, and others, as well as respect for our elders, leaders, and superiors. We were definitely not permitted to call the name of the Lord in vain. If we were heard saying, "Oh God," we received a strong reprimand. My mother's form of discipline was usually to deny us the privilege of going to places or doing something that we loved, such as going to the beach or going out with friends.

My mother was a gentle and loving person who definitely put our needs before hers. She was also very close to her biological family. This meant that we always had to walk for miles to visit her cousins, nieces, and nephews, who lived on the other side of the Island. When any of them came to visit and spend the night, one or other of us had to give him or her our bed and sleep on the floor. Our home also seemed to be a "house of refuge" for some other nieces and nephews who lived in the same village as we did. When they ran into problems at home, they would come to her and she would take them to their homes and intercede for them. She encouraged us to serve and help the elderly and the sick, and she always seemed to share what provisions we had with others. One memory of my early childhood, apart from playing hide and seek, telling and listening to anancy stories, or having to make up my own story to tell on a moonlit night as we sat outside with her as a family, is that of having the responsibility of accompanying an elderly neighbour every month to make sure that she received her pension.

Together, my parents tried to raise us in the, "fear of the Lord." During my childhood and early youth, however, I did not fully understand what that meant. In addition to teaching us that we must love God, love one another, and the family, and that we must respect our elders, they taught us to say "Please," "Thank you," and "Sorry, please forgive me." They emphasized the importance of hard work and the value of honesty, discipline, and obedience. "Trust and obey," was a favourite song at our house. We were each assigned a chore, such as making up our bed, sweeping the yard, washing dishes, or cleaning and tidying the house, on a daily or weekly basis, and held accountable for its achievement. A washerwoman did our washing, but we had to take the clothes to her and pick them up again. I remember my younger sister falling into a river once on her way back from collecting the laundry. She was taking a short cut. What is remarkable is that she told no one. She simply brought the basket with the wet laundry home, placed it on the back step and went to bed. You can imagine my mother's reaction when she found the wet laundry the next day! Needless to say, my younger sister was nowhere to be found on that day.

Roman Catholicism was, and still is not a dominant religion on our island. During my youth, there was only one priest to service the available churches. Mass was, therefore, said in our village on the first and third Sundays of the month, either at 7.00 a.m. or 9.00 a.m. My parents made sure that we, their children, attended Mass on those two Sundays. My father supported this. However, because he had no one to accompany him to the Methodist church, he sometimes bemoaned the fact that he had promised the priest, at their marriage, that he would let our mother raise us as Catholics. Despite this, however, he made sure that we were all at the foot of their bed each morning to say the Rosary, and he would clean our shoes on a Sunday morning to be sure that we were well presented. He loved cleaning shoes! He would sing while cleaning the shoes.

As a family, we were not materially wealthy, but we had sufficient to live on and to share. For example, when pigeon peas was in season, my mother always sent some for her sister or for elderly persons who could no longer engage in gardening. Additionally, my mother always cooked more than was needed by the household. She would then send one of us to give some to an old person or relative or offer some to anyone passing by in front of the house, on his or her way home from his or her garden. I think a few of them looked forward to that! Thus, as they neared the house, they would call out her name loudly, and ask how she was doing. Even as children, we could decipher the message!

Having excess when others had none, as well as wastage was a "No, no." We had to share. We had to eat what was on our plate and were constantly reminded of the starving children in China. I often wondered how eating all my food could benefit the starving children in China, but I never asked. That would have been too "cheeky" or rude. Later in life, I realized that they were telling me that even though we had said grace before meals, I must remain eternally grateful and not waste, because there were others who were starving. When I finally understood that, I added to the grace I was taught, "Remember Lord those who have none, especially the children." I still say that. Through my upbringing, I am not surprised that as I grew older, I became and remain a member of the St Vincent de Paul Society, a society within the Catholic church that is dedicated to the care of the aged, poor, sick, needy, prisoners, and other less fortunate persons. As society members, we try to see Christ in our neighbour and to serve them as referred to in Matthew 25:31-45. I feel blessed that I have been able to serve in this way in most of the countries in which I have been privileged to reside.

My early childhood years spanned World War 2. That meant that rationing of foodstuff such as sugar and rice was in place. My parents grew all the food we ate. This included the making of sugar. My father grew sugar cane, squeezed the juice and boiled it in a large copper until it became a form of sugar. Villagers purchased this. During this time also, there were no credit cards. The over-riding philosophy that was passed on to us as children, was that we must live within our means and always save something for a rainy day.

1.2: My Siblings

Each of my siblings played important roles in my childhood and in my life's journey. I was the sixth of the eight children of my parents. Without the benefit of knowledge of family planning, my mother breast- fed each of us for two years and had us three years apart. Thus, by the time I came along, some of my older siblings were already adults. This was great for me, because my eldest sister literally took me under her wings. She loved me and protected me; she hugged and kissed me, and made sure that I always had enough to eat. She would bathe me, comb my hair, and prepare me for going to school. When I was leaving for school, she would say to me, "Now learn the lessons for the two of us, eh." She loved me and I loved her. Her love was a positive motivator, as love always is. I tried to return that love and it has been very satisfying and rewarding. Even now at the old age of 85 years, I am able to return to Tobago, after all my travels and widowhood, and reside, free of charge, in the apartment I had constructed to accommodate her, so as to have her closer to me upon her husband's death and her failing health.

My senior brother was 11 years older than I. He always made me laugh. He always teased me. Sometimes he would ask me for the meat on my plate. When I refused, he would say, "Remember, you have to give to get!" As a child, I could not see what I would get by giving him my meat! However, by the time he was about to leave home, when I was 10 years old, I had learned to turn the tables. At that time, however, I did not fully understand what he was teaching me. I thought that he just wanted my meat! That lesson, that I have to give to get, has now become a part of my psyche and is one of my life's guidelines. After he left home, he always sent money to help my mother to pay my high-school fees. He even helped to pay my passage as I left Tobago to pursue my career in England. I owe him so much. Unfortunately, I have never been able to repay his love. However, I learned to pass it on to other members of my family as well as to others, as I came to realize that I could not claim to love them without reaching out to them as I perceived their area of need. The sayings, "Love is not love until it is given away," and, "It is more blessed to give than to receive," are true and bring immeasurable satisfaction.

My other senior siblings were also loving, caring and responsible. One took me to live with her and her family so I could go to High school in San Fernando, on the sister island of Trinidad. From my siblings, I learned that I had a responsibility to look out for those who came after me. I hope that I have succeeded in so doing. My family would have to attest to that, but I think that the response would be positive. I was the first to travel outside of Trinidad and Tobago and was instrumental in getting a younger sister to England and now have nieces, great and grand nieces and nephews who are British born citizens. I was also instrumental in getting nieces and nephews to Canada, and now also have great nieces and nephews who are Canadian born citizens. I mention this because I never became a biological mother. Nonetheless, I feel blessed beyond measure because of the special place I hold in the hearts of these members of the family, and the love we share.

My siblings continue to help in my spiritual growth. For example, one of the nephews who joined me in Canada decided to get married. I decided to present him with a monetary gift which I suggested that he should use towards buying a house. He decided to use it to buy a new car. I was livid. I did not think that there was anything wrong with his old car, so, I complained to his mother, one of my older sisters. Her response was that I should thank the Lord that I had it to give! I became furious with her as well. When I calmed down and reflected on it, I came to the realization that she was right. It was through God's grace that I had the money to give, and my nephew was accountable to God and not to me. As a child of God, I was expected to share with others what He had so generously given to me, without expecting anything in return. This made a great impact on my future behaviour. A summary of the extent to which I was able to pass on the love and gifts I received from God to others outside my biological family, is recorded in Chapter 7: Legacy.

As I reflect on my early life, I cannot help but affirm that, "The HOME is indeed the "DOMESTIC CHURCH." Our Parents may not be perfect, but they love us and would/should not lead us astray. "God is love." Remember!!! At our early age, parents certainly have the responsibility to act, "in Persona Christi" to teach us the road we should follow, even though as we grow older we may choose not to follow for one reason or another. *MY PRAYER is that all parents recognize the important role that they play in the life of their children and take that responsibility seriously. I thank the Lord for the parents and siblings He gave me. I pray also for those who have no parents, or who have only a single parent, that the Good Lord will send them suitable surrogate parents, at least in their early childhood.*

Siblings

1.3: The Extended Family

As you would have gathered, I had my fair share of uncles, aunts, and cousins. Some were kind and loving, but some of my father's family had "*shade*" issues. They were mixed race and called mulattos or bacras. They had a light colour with long, soft, curly hair and one sister, in particular, did not seem to like us because we were too black. The majority were, however, loving and kind and treated us as their own. I fondly remember one of my father's brothers whom we nicknamed, "Uncle Small Change." This was because every time we met him, he would say, "Leh me see if I have any small change to give you." Then, he would go into his pocket and take out a penny and give it to us so we could buy sweetie or lollipop. As young children, we loved that. It was nice running into him.

I also remember Papa Sam. He was my mother's first cousin, but like a brother to her. His children all called my mother, "Auntie Nora." While in high school in Tobago, every lunchtime I would go out to his joiner shop and he always had some advice for me. His two younger sons were around my age and were like my brothers. They were always there for me. They looked out for me. One even took me along with him when he was courting a young lady who later became his wife. Her parents would not let her leave their house alone with him, but he seemed to be able to persuade them that she was safe when I was along with them. We grew up at a time when the ships, steamers, transporting passengers between our twin islands had to anchor off-shore at the Scarborough harbour. Papa Sam owned boats that took passengers from the wharf to the steamer. Whenever either of my cousins was home from school in Trinidad, and even after they graduated and were awaiting employment, they would take me on rides to and from the steamer. I enjoyed that, and we remained very close. I was even called from my residence in Washington D.C. to be at the younger brother's bedside and hold his hand as he died. The second brother prepared a room for me in his marital home, so that whenever I was in Tobago, I had to spend some time with him and his family.

When I was leaving home, Tobago, for Canada, I remember Papa Sam saying to me, "Look out for the others, remember water can only rise to its own level." I understood him to be saying that it did not matter how far I would rise in the world, if other people could point at members in my family as non-achievers, then they were pointing at me, so I had a responsibility to help others in the family. He gave me the address of his son, my cousin, who was a doctor in Canada. He was nine years older than I, received his education in Trinidad and left there even before I entered high school, so I really did not know him as well as I did his younger brothers. However, all I had to do was contact him, tell him who I was, and that Papa Sam had given me his address, and that was it. He took me as a sister into his marital family and I became his children's auntie. I even ran afoul of his eldest daughter when in answer to her enquiry about what her father was like as a child, l tried to get her to understand that we were not biological siblings. She became very adamant. Of course, I was her aunt and Mamie, my mother, whom she met when she spent some time in Canada, was indeed her grandmother. I dropped the subject. My family ties were that close.

1.4: The Community

Tobago, the island of my birth and early nurturing, is the smaller island of the twin island state of Trinidad and Tobago. It had a population of only forty thousand during my younger days, even though like ours, families were large. It can hardly be seen on a standard sized world map. Its economy was mainly agricultural and marine based. There are no known mineral resources. Those not wishing to work in agriculture generally migrated to Trinidad, Aruba or Venezuela to work in the oil or related industry. It is, however, one of the most beautiful islands in the world. One of the tourist brochures describes it as, "Clean, Green and Serene," and so it is.

When I was growing up, the population was about 99% of African descent. The other 1% was constituted of Chinese, Syrians, Whites, East Indians, and persons of mixed races. It is basically a safe island, with a minimum of violence and crime. During my childhood, I can remember only two murders on the island. Praedial larceny seemed to have been the main crime. Some persons were identified as thieves and we were warned to avoid them. The young were advised not to marry into those families. People basically expressed their disagreement and anger by "cussing out" (cursing) their opponent and "falling out" with them (no longer talking to them.) Bye and large, Tobagonians are warm, friendly, hospitable, caring and supportive of one another. Christianity is the main religion on the island. The majority of the population are, however, Protestants, and unlike our sister island of Trinidad, Roman Catholics are in the minority. However, as young Catholics, we had the privilege of having our own catechist at the school each morning. This has influenced my life and is reflected in my writing. However, I do believe that God loves us all and as long as we believe in Him and that Jesus is Lord, to the Glory of God the Father; we are all brothers and sisters, thus what He has done for me He can do for anyone, regardless of his or her religious affiliation.

During my childhood, the island was not very developed. Only the capital city had access to electricity, potable water, and a sewage disposal system. We lived 3 miles outside of the city. The Island experiences two rainy seasons and two dry seasons annually. My father provided us with a water tank that collected water from the roof during the rainy seasons. If it ran dry before the rains came again, we did what the majority of villagers did. We went to the river to fetch water and have a bath before going to school. We enjoyed this. We swam in the river and spent time looking under the rocks for crayfish which we took home to eat. We used "Pit" latrines. In the rural areas, lighting was provided through kerosene (pitch oil) lamps or candles. This is how we did our homework, so, we did it early and went to bed, except on moonlight nights. There was no television at that time, so, on moonlight nights, we sat on the steps and told "Anancy" stories, or ones we had created by ourselves, or sang. Sometimes we played "riddles" or "hide and seek," or "hopscotch."

Obtaining a secondary education at that time was also a challenge. There was only one recognized high school, Bishop's High School, on the island. It was started and administered by the Anglican Church, but was basically non-sectarian. It did not exist when my parents were children. There was a great demand for admission to high school, therefore, most parents who wanted their children to receive secondary education, had to send them to the sister island of Trinidad. This was costly. Additionally, scholarships were few and far between thus many children with the ability to benefit from a higher level of education were left behind. This was mainly because the majority of Tobagonians, at that time, were either mainly involved in subsistence farming or worked for the larger landowners on their "estates" and had limited cash income. As a result, mainly only those whose parents were in commerce, owned properties or businesses, were fishermen or public servants, were able to get educated at the secondary level.

The island is comprised of several villages. In those days, each village had its own personality and accent. One could invariably tell which village a person was from by his or her speech. Persons in a village generally looked out for, or looked after one another. Sharing was common place. Additionally, everyone in the village knew everyone else, and I must add, everyone else's business. They, therefore, felt that they could advise the young on who to avoid as "bad company." Marriages either took place within the village, or men would take wives from outside the village and bring them to their village. Men did not generally move out of their village of birth. This meant that one could accurately guess the village a person was from by his or her surname. Inheritance was basically through the male.

Villages operated independently of one another. Despite this, however, there was a feeling of kinship throughout the island. This seemed to have been nurtured by the Churches, and was evidenced each year when persons travelled from one part of the island to the next at "Harvest" time, to support the various churches and to entertain, or be entertained, by the particular community. Through this practice, some strong inter-village bonds were formed.

Transportation was mainly by government buses, which generally ran at fixed times and only during the day. As a student, if you missed the first bus, to the city in the morning, your only choice was to walk. This meant that you would be late for school and risk detention after school. If you missed the last bus in the evening, your choice was either to walk or take one of the few taxis from the capital. These were expensive and risky for young girls. One thus learnt to be on time. Punctuality was thus built into our daily lives. Walking three or four miles to try to get home in the evening before dark was no fun. Remember there were no street- lights outside of the city.

My most remarkable memory of the community in which I was raised is that all seniors saw themselves as my parents. This gave them the right to correct me, or to report me to my parents for further discipline, if I was in any way rude to them, or if they saw me with others whom they considered "bad company." The community, nonetheless, nurtured a sense of belonging, since there was also sharing and caring. Whenever there was any disagreement between my parents and any member of the family or community, we were strongly admonished to, "Stay out of it." We were to show the customary respect and not attempt to take sides.

There was a wisdom in the community which the older people strove to impart to us, the younger ones, to strengthen, guide, and protect us. In a similar manner, through my early religious teaching, some of these guidelines became ingrained in my psyche and would rise to the surface at appropriate times. Some were said in the Queen's English and some in the local parlance. Examples include: "All skin teeth nuh good laugh." When translated, that says that not everyone who smiles with you is genuine and to be trusted.

Others included: "Honesty is the best policy." "Do suh nuh like suh." Translated this means that those who do you wrong do not like you to do the same to them, so do unto others as you would have them do unto you. There were also, "Show me your companion and I'll tell yuh your character," and "Birds of a feather flock together," both of which are telling us to beware of the company we keep because that is the yardstick by which others would judge us. Some of the ones which I found particularly helpful on my life's journey are: " God doesn't sleep;" "Out of evil cometh good;" "Beggars can't be choosers;" "Don't count yuh chickens before they are hatched;" "Yuh have to creep before yuh walk;" " Wha nuh meet yuh nuh pass yuh." This means that you should not judge others because you do not know what you would do in the same situation. Still others were, "Never put off for tomorrow what you can do today," and, " Who don't hear does feel." This last one indicated that you must listen to your elders and instructions including the commandments and the voice of God, otherwise be prepared for the consequences.

I can definitely say that the community in which I grew up played a very nurturing and positive role in my upbringing. I thank the Lord for that. The saying, "It takes a village to raise a child," was certainly applied during my childhood.

Together, my parents, my siblings, my village community and Church provided the foundation and prepared me for my life's journey. As a child I felt loved.

1.5: Primary Education

I entered school at age 5 years. There was only one primary school in our village– the Mason Hall Government School. All children were expected to attend school. Parents were required to ensure that their children arrived at school on time. Truancy was discouraged.

Religious education was part of the school's program. A catechist came every morning to teach the fundamentals of the Roman Catholic religion to the catholic children. I cannot remember or recall all that she taught us. I do, however, remember her telling us that we were children of God; that God loved us; that the Virgin Mary was our mother whom Jesus had given to those whom he loved, as he was dying on the cross; that she also loved us; that the Church was started by Jesus and that we should show Him that we love Him by always saying our prayers, going to Mass, going to confession, receiving forgiveness and being good and kind to one another. We were also taught the ten commandments and told to obey them. Two other teachings remained with me. These were two basic questions. The first was, "Who made you?" The answer, "God made me." The second question was, "Why did God make you?" The answer, "God made me to know him, love him and serve him in this world, and be with him forever in the next." That was good for a child to know, but what exactly did it all mean? I did not fully understand it then, but it stuck with me like the sum, "2+2=4." Fortunately, I was later able to understand it. This was part of my foundation and comes back to me regularly when I contemplate on the nature and quality of my service, and periodically, when I must address issues such as abortion and euthanasia.

During my first two years at school, it seems that I manifested some signs of a learning disability. For example, whereas I was exceptionally good at Mental Arithmetic and could get the correct answer mentally, whenever I had to write the answers down on paper, I wrote the numbers backwards. I seem to have had the same problem with spelling. That bothered my stage three teacher, who was at a loss as to how to help. On one of his visits, the School Inspector, Mr. Sealy, advised her not to worry too much because I would grow out of it. I obviously did, because I was promoted to Standard One, skipped Standard Two, moved to Standard Three, then Standard Four and instead of going to Standard Five, I was put in "Special Class." This was a class in which students were prepared to write the examination for scholarships for admission to high school. I did well and although I did not obtain a scholarship, my parents were able to get me into Naparima Girls High school on the sister isle of Trinidad.

At primary school, I became a Brownee. I had fun playing hop-scotch and other games with my friends. I liked being involved in relays, three-legged race, and other sports on Sport days. I enjoyed running. Whether or not I was competing with others, it seems that I was always running. I ran to school, ran home for lunch, ran back to school, ran to church, and everywhere that I was sent. As I grew older, I moved to jogging. Now at the ripe old age of eighty-five I have graduated to walking slowly. However, I still firmly believe in the importance of daily physical movement.

1.6: Secondary Education

1.6.1: Naparima Girls High School (NGHS)

NGHS was a Presbyterian High School and we started the day with devotions. At that time, religious knowledge was a basic course and what I learnt then became part of my foundation and life reference. I remember learning the 23rd Psalm, "The Lord is my Shepherd," Psalm 27, "The Lord is my light and my salvation; whom shall I fear," and Psalm 91, "He that dwelleth in the secret place of the most high shall abide in the shadow of the almighty." These all became part of my mainstay. I would reflect on them whenever I was in any kind of difficulty and they re-assured me. We also studied "The Acts of the Apostles."

At NGHS I had my first real encounter with East Indians of my age group, and I made a few very good friends among them. In Tobago, I was only aware of the presence of one East Indian family and it did not seem to have any girls in my age group. There were also students from other ethnic and cultural backgrounds, and I began to understand and accept people from other cultures. This put me on the road to endorsing multiculturalism.

My time at NGHS was not altogether positive. On the negative side, I developed a complex that has, to this day, affected my ability or willingness to learn a foreign language. This was by no means because of the method of teaching at the school. Somehow or the other, I seemed to have failed to understand the concepts of conjugation and declension. Thus, at the end of the first term, I obtained minus four out of fifty, as my mark for Latin and I saw myself as a "language dunce." Although my marks improved after that, I really have never gotten over my negative attitude towards learning other languages.

I am by nature a very social animal. I enjoyed being involved in sporting events, being able to go to the beach on weekends, going to dances, and visiting with family and family friends. These events were not available to me at NGHS. Additionally, when I entered NGHS, there were no other children from Tobago at the school, and there seemed to be an atmosphere of social discrimination or differentiation. I felt like a foreigner. Thus, even though I was able to make some friends, and lived with an older sister and her family, I felt lonely and did not adjust very well. I missed my Tobago lifestyle, my parents and eldest sister. Finally, I was able to persuade my mother to get me back to school in Tobago.

1.6.2: *Bishops High School* (BHS), Tobago.

BHS was an Anglican school and again we started each day with devotions. Without realizing it, my education was making me a multi-cultural, multi-denominational person. Rev. Jones, who was the Principal at the time, was very fond of the hymn, "Father we thank thee for the night and for the pleasant morning bright." It seems that we sang it at least once every week. I liked that hymn and would sing it, even to this day, as part of my morning devotions. Additionally, I learnt a number of other Anglican hymns which, by God's grace, I was able to sing to and with my Anglican husband on his deathbed. *Everything happens for the best and for this I am very grateful.*

At BHS in Tobago, I became more involved in sports and other school and after school activities, such as debating and playing netball. I also made lifelong friends. I became a "Girl guide," and it was reinforced that I must always strive for excellence, do my best, be prepared, and help others. I became a class prefect and I graduated with a second grade Cambridge School Certificate. During my adolescence, however, my thoughts and orientation were mainly on my educational preparation, socialization and on myself. I enjoyed going to beach outings with my friends and participating in all the normal activities of youth. I may even have gone over the line in terms of what I thought was fun in desiring to be accepted by my peers. Fortunately for me, the community, my family, and Church enabled me to survive the difficult period of adolescence.

All In all, I had a very happy, fulfilling and satisfying childhood and adolescence. I thank God that even though I did not have as much or as many material items as some of my peers, I had the love of my family and His love. He obviously loved me more than I loved myself even though I did not realize it at the time.

Maybe, as I would keep on mentioning the Lord and thanking Him, some young people might think that I was a religious zealot or a "goodie two shoes," or a freak who did not have fun and enjoy life. As you continue to read on, however, I hope you would understand why thanking the Lord became and remains such an important part of my journey through life, as I acknowledge that I am a sinner whom the Lord loves and never seems to cease to forgive. My life has really been a love story.

2

THE JOURNEY CONTINUES: INTELLECTUAL, PROFESSIONAL, SOCIAL AND SPIRITUAL GROWTH

2.1: Entry into Nursing. *My Student Years in England -1955 to 1962.*

During my adolescence, I wanted to become a pharmacist or a teacher. There was, however, no formal career guidance programme at school and I had difficulty deciding on a profession. However, as I can now firmly attest, one of the mysterious ways in which God works is by speaking through other simple, trustworthy people. This is one of the most common ways through which He has spoken to and guided me throughout my life. All I have had to do was to be willing and able to LISTEN and discern His voice. Like all Christians, my call was to serve God. However, it took me some time to recognize that and to determine how I was to go about doing so. Even during my thirties, I remember a "Poor Clare" nun suggesting that I should join that order, but I knew that I was neither disciplined nor obedient enough to join a religious order. God knew that too. He was grooming and blessing me with a successful career and work life that enabled me to serve Him at the same time. It is remarkable how both aspects came together so naturally without one detracting from the other. They rather strengthened each other. And as you would see, the more I grew in faith and service, the more my career flourished and vice versa.

As mentioned earlier, I thought that I wanted to become a pharmacist or a teacher. Upon graduation from high school, however, I was a little confused.

I can now see that the idea was MY WILL, not GOD'S WILL for me, and my confusion was because I was not yet able to discern that He was saying "WAIT." Soon after graduation from high school, I went to visit relatives in South Trinidad. While there, I contacted a friend who had become a student nurse. She suggested that I should join the nursing profession. She said that I had all the qualities of a good nurse and that I should apply to the Nursing school at the San Fernando General Hospital. I had never given any thought to becoming a nurse, and the thought of having to work at night was not very appealing to me. I did, however, follow my friend, Nestor's, advice and that was obviously God's will for me. I have never regretted taking that advice seriously.

I started off as a student nurse at the San Fernando General hospital and was enjoying it. Soon after my entry, however, a new matron was appointed at the hospital. She came from England and she was black! Oh! I thought, there are opportunities in England for black nurses! My love and desire to travel and see the world "kicked in." I decided to go to England and see for myself. So, off to England I went. I did not know at the time that I was setting out on a journey that would enable me to grow educationally, psychologically, socially and spiritually, and to see more of the world than I could ever have dreamt.

My mother saw me off at the jetty in Trinidad. She was happy but concerned. She advised me to be good and to remember to pray and go to church. She hugged and kissed me. When I looked back at her, as I mounted the gangway, there were tears in her eyes. I knew then that I had to succeed for her sake.

In Barcelona en-route to England

The journey to England was enlightening. I made friends with another young lady who was also travelling to England to study Nursing. The steamer on which we travelled stopped in Tenerife, in the Canary Islands, then in Barcelona in Spain. We were allowed to disembark in both places and did a short tour of the cities. We then went on to Genoa in Italy where we disembarked and were transferred by train over the Alps to Calais, France. From there we boarded the ferry to England. I was met at Kings Cross Station by a representative from the hospital.

2.2. Saxondale Hospital

The hospital to which I had applied and was accepted, was a "Mental hospital!" I did not realize this when I left Trinidad. I am not sure that I would have made the decision to go there had I known. I am also not sure whether my parents would have embraced the idea of my going there either. At that time the popular belief was that a mental hospital was a "madhouse," where crazy and dangerous people were put so that the public would be protected from them. The fact that a person with mental problems can recover and make a meaningful contribution to society was then not known to me. When I arrived at the hospital, however, I loved it. There were other students there from the Caribbean, and everyone, including the staff on the ward on which I was placed, was friendly and warm. The training opened my eyes to a deep understanding and acceptance of human behaviour, including my own. It also set me off on a career path that I would not have imagined. GOD DOES INDEED WORK IN MYSTERIOUS WAYS!

I arrived in England in the mid-1950s. At that time there was a heavy migration of persons from Commonwealth countries to the United Kingdom, and those of us who chose the health professions were welcomed. At the beginning of my studies in England, my intellectual growth was inextricably linked to my emotional and psycho-social growth. The first growth challenge that I had on arrival in England was that of resolving issues related to my racial identity and determining who I was. Who is Margaret Price? On reflection, I think that I had a slight complex about my colour when I left Tobago. In Trinidad and Tobago at that time, which was during the colonial era, there was a form of colour prejudice. Even among the black population "Shades" of black were important. If you were "brown skin" or "light skin" you were "IN." This extended even to obtaining a job at a bank. Experiences in England contributed to the disappearance of any complex I might have had about my colour, and gave me the strength to just BE ME. In England, if you were black, you were black. We were all called "Negroes", and "Shades" did not seem to matter. Additionally, I observed three situations that taught me that hatred of or the desire to be different, or in some way superior to others, was deeply embedded in the recesses of man's heart or his being.

The first observation which affected me was of "white on white" discrimination. Every Sunday I joined other Roman Catholic nurses and nursing students to walk to Mass in the nearby village. Without exception, every Sunday morning, the Catholics from Northern Ireland and those from Southern Ireland had arguments and made disparaging remarks about each other. They never seemed to be friends. That was disturbing to me. They were both Catholics, both white, both from the same island, and yet they seemed to have an unreasonable dislike for each other. I did not understand their politics and what was behind their behaviour. Both groups were very nice and supportive of me and I was thus invited to and able to visit both Northern and Southern Ireland. There, I also found out about the Catholic/Protestant divide. I thus concluded that hatred and prejudice did not limit itself to colour.

This conclusion was reinforced by a second observation when I went to the General Hospital as part of my training. There, after the war, many of us came from different parts of the Commonwealth. We did not exactly like the English food. Except perhaps for fish and chips and roast beef and Yorkshire pudding, we found the food too bland. A group of us, therefore, decided that on our "days-off," we would cook our native food and share it among ourselves. In the group, there were two students from the island of Cyprus, one Greek and one Turkish in origin. Whenever the Greek Cypriot student cooked, the Turkish Cypriot student would not eat, and vice versa. Why this? I asked myself. Both were good cooks! The rest of us were eating their cooked food and enjoying and surviving it!

A third eye-opener was "Tribalism." Coming from a small homogenous island, I had never seen or experienced this before. To me at the time, all Nigerians were Nigerians. However, I came to realize that there were tribal differences between the "Igbo" and the "Yoruba" students. They were both black, both Africans and from the same country, but they did not mix.

These examples, coupled with my experience with issues related to "shades of black" and differential relationships between Hindus and Muslims, that existed in my own country, made me realize that discrimination, hatred, and prejudice were problems of mankind throughout the world, and that there was really nothing I could do about them. There was, therefore, no point in my worrying about who does not like me because of my colour, because human beings seemed to be able to find endless reasons for disliking or wanting to "put down" one another. What is more important is that, as I was taught in my early catechism, God made me, and He loves. He, therefore, must have had a good reason for making me black. I cannot say what that reason is, but it must be a good one, because AS THE OLD PEOPLE IN THE VILLAGE USED TO SAY, "GOD DOES NOT MAKE MISTAKES." I, therefore, concluded that if someone does not like me because of my colour or race it is his or her problem, not mine. Obviously, unless I have done something hurtful to that person, I cannot be responsible for what is in that person's heart, or how that person feels. I, therefore, made a lifelong decision never to internalize any negative emotions, or pay attention to anyone who takes exception to my colour, or my height, or my size, or my country, or anything that he or she chooses not to like, but to remain true to myself, be happy and keep smiling.

The introduction to the study of psychology as part of my training was instrumental in reinforcing my decision not to pay attention to negative persons. I also realized that a person who is nasty or abusive, expects a negative response, including fear and/or subservience. I adopted the principle of counting to ten before responding to any perceived negativity. I realized that when I respond positively or with a smile it throws people with negative thoughts off balance; so, I keep smiling. I also accepted the reality that God has made us all equal, so no one is better than me and vice versa. I, therefore, also decided never to "Lord" it over anyone. That to me, would make me no better than the person who is trying to hurt, humiliate, intimidate or belittle me. That decision has paid great dividends.

Since then, whenever I experience instances of subtle or blatant discrimination, I just do not let them hold me back. If I cannot deal with the situation head on, without becoming negative or bitter, I say a short prayer asking God to strengthen me or to intercede, and I seek ways to go around that experience, or distance myself from it. I simply do not let negativity spoil my joy. From my childhood, I have always smiled, and that has worked wonders in helping me to overcome challenges. My smile has also been a positive factor in drawing others to me and helping others to relax in my presence. It is an ability that I hope I would never lose. To me, it is a God- given gift. It comes from the heart and others see it.

I have experienced several instances of discrimination on my life's journey. Some were racial, some sexual, and some were even professional. However, when I recognize them for what they are, I have managed to never let them hold me back. As a matter of fact, these instances have been stimuli to make me do better. They have strengthened my faith in the power of prayer. *For example,* as a student at the Mental hospital, I experienced a subtle form of discrimination from one of my two male tutors. I do not know whether it was because I was female, because I was black, or because I was coming from a "third world" country. As a student, I was required to do my preliminary training or PTS. I had already done this in Trinidad, so I was ahead of the others. However, even though all my answers were correct, I was never able to score 100% or be first in the class in the subject that he taught. There would always be a male student who would be put one point ahead of me, even though he had incorrect answers. I never became bitter or resentful. I was determined to work harder to see what he would do. I did not complain, I was there to qualify as a nurse, not to prove that he was a racist or a male chauvinist. I consoled myself with the fact that as long as he was not failing me, and would not be the one correcting the Board examinations, I could live with what he was doing. I gave him all the respect related to his position. I would smile and thank him for his assistance, and in the end, I won the war. He became a strong supporter. He selected me to be among the first batch of four students to be enrolled in the newly instituted four- year integrated programme of Mental and General Nursing. This enabled me to obtain both my State Registered Nursing (SRN) and my Registered Mental Nursing (RMN) certificates in four years, instead of five.

I believe that I could have lost if I had gone into battle with him every time that I thought that he had been unfair to me. He was the Principal

Tutor. I could have been type-casted as having a negative attitude or worse, and that could have hindered my progress. There are times when one has to 'stoop to conquer.'

Interestingly enough, the male student who the principal tutor insisted on putting ahead of me, knew what was going on. He would always ask to see my paper, show me his, and we would smile! We became very good friends. He invited me home to meet his parents, introduced me to his fiancé, and they both usually invited me to go along with them to shows and concerts. They took me to my first experience of Handel's Messiah at a Concert Hall. We remained friends. He was also chosen for, and completed the four-year integrated programme.

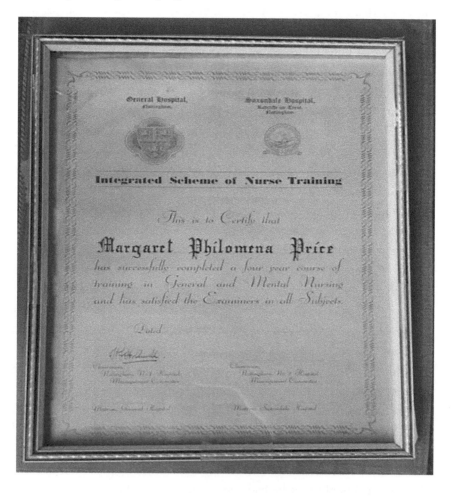

2.3: Nottingham General Hospital (NGH).

At the NGH, I was very impressed with the role that Ward Sisters (Head Nurses) played in the education of both Medical and Nursing students. They were strict but made sure that we each had opportunities to learn. Each morning, as the report of the previous night's activities was shared, a student would be asked what he or she knew about a diagnosis and the possible treatment and nursing care. You, therefore, had to keep up-to-date or be publicly embarrassed. It meant, however, that you did not have to "cram" or engage in a lot of last-minute studying for examinations, as long as there were patients with different diagnoses on the wards to which you were assigned. Additionally, senior doctors provided information in their field of specialization and contributed to the relevant examination in their area of expertise. In our first year of rotation at the General Hospital, I won the Surgical Nursing prize. This made our group of four really happy.

Recipient of the Surgical Nursing Award at the NGH

When we had first arrived at the General hospital, we were made to feel that one only needed 'brawn' (strong muscles) not brains, to be a mental nurse. Thus, we were treated by other students as if we were inferior. I studied hard and proved them wrong by receiving the Surgical Nursing award. Our small group felt that my achievement was proof that mental nurses also had brains.

Our entire group continued doing well during our general hospital rotations, and I believe that that one achievement of mine succeeded, not only in motivating the others, but in gaining respect for our group. I knew who I was. I was a winner and I was not going to let others define me. Another member of our group received the Orthopaedic Nursing prize the next year. We each completed the course and became State Registered genera Nurses (SRNs) as well as Registered Mental Nurses (RMNs), the first group to achieve this in four years.

Social growth

During my rotation at the General hospital, I met and made many good friends from different nationalities and cultures, including persons from other Caribbean islands, from Africa, Germany, Cyprus, Persia (Iran), India, and from as far away as Hong Kong. I was able to go to dances at the Palais, go to the theatre and to the movies and enjoyed myself. I met handsome young men from Africa and the Caribbean, as well as from England. I was, however, not very adventurous. I neither drank nor smoked. As a child, I had witnessed drunkenness among some family members and in the community and decided that I would never drink alcohol. Additionally, I could see where that was leading some of my friends. We were far away from home, with a degree of freedom that most, if not all of us, never previously had. We were all lonely to a certain extent. We missed our families and our cultures. Some of us filled the void by spending the days-off with boyfriends. The outcomes were not always favourable. Additionally, I always looked younger than my age and for some reason most of the guys I met saw me as their little sister or just a friend who was a good dancer and who needed protection. One even wanted to know how old one had to be to get into nursing, because at age

20, I looked like I was about 14 years old. I was skinny. I was 5'6" tall, but I weighed just between 100 to 110 pounds.

For some reason that I still cannot explain, I never felt lonely. I joined a book club and received monthly publications, which I read assiduously. Additionally, my mother seemed to be always with me. Although she was far away in Tobago, I never wanted to disappoint or hurt her. She had worked so hard and sacrificed so much to get me to where I was, so, it was always: "What would Mamie say if I did this, or if I did that?" If my inner voice told me that she would not approve, I refrained from engaging in that particular action. I later realized that that was God protecting me by keeping my mother at the centre of my being.

My mother and I kept in constant contact. During my early days in England, for as long as she could get away with putting an item in the mail, she would send it to me. She sent parcels with things such as cod liver oil, corn flour, Ferrol Compound, local bene balls and anything that she remembered that I liked. It took some time before I was eventually able to persuade her that I was fine and could get most of those things in England. When I graduated, my desire to return home was prompted, in great part, by my desire to see her. When I migrated to Canada, I was happy to be able to have her come for a visit and stay with me for a while. When she was dying, she asked for me. I was blessed with the opportunity of getting to Tobago on time to see her for about three hours before she died, and to be at her bedside holding her hand as she passed on to eternity. She was definitely a "Sweet Mother," and I can never forget her. She went, but, left me in God's hands. All that she had tried to teach me about love of God took on deeper meaning, and I returned to the daily recitation of and meditation on the Rosary, in addition to daily prayers of thanksgiving.

My experience at the General Hospital was quite rewarding. I learnt a lot in the two years. I got used to being on night duty. The only negative experience was that I got sick whenever I was on the paediatric ward. I seem to contract every infection that the children brought in. Thus, my paediatric experience was shortened. When I arrived in Canada, the time spent on paediatrics during my training was said to be too short and I was asked to write the paediatric nursing examination. I was writing that examination on the day that President Kennedy was assassinated. I can never forget that. I was traumatised. However, I was able to pass the examination.

During my stay in Nottinghamshire as a student, I was able to holiday in Scotland, Ireland and Wales. I remained at Saxondale Hospital for two years after graduation, and was made a Deputy sister in the second year. However, I felt a strong urge to train as a midwife and return home to Trinidad and Tobago.

2.4: Midwifery Training.

I was blessed and honoured to be admitted to Guy's hospital, which was one of the most prestigious hospitals in London, to receive the first part of my midwifery training. I completed the second part of my midwifery training at Hackney Hospital. By this time, I had two sisters and brothers in law, as well two nieces in London. Most of my days off were, therefore, happily spent with family. Other days were spent visiting places of interest around London and enjoying rides in the double-decker buses or the underground (Tube). I was able to see Buckingham Palace and the changing of the guards, the houses of Parliament, Leicester Square and other places of interest, as well as plays at Covent Gardens.

Outside Buckingham Palace

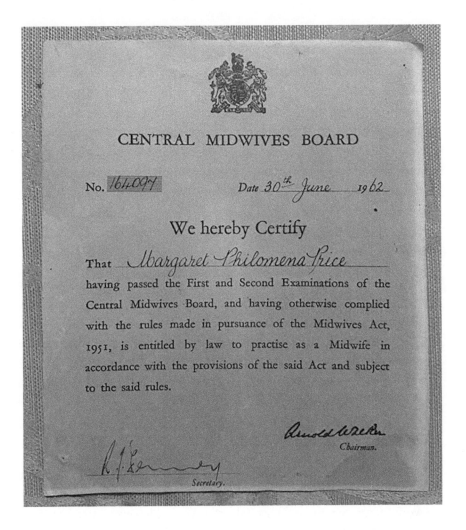

CENTRAL MIDWIVES BOARD

No. *164097*   Date *30ᵗʰ June   1962*

We hereby Certify

That ___*Margaret Philomena Price*___

having passed the First and Second Examinations of the Central Midwives Board, and having otherwise complied with the rules made in pursuance of the Midwives Act, 1951, is entitled by law to practise as a Midwife in accordance with the provisions of the said Act and subject to the said rules.

Arnold Walker
Chairman.

R.J. Kenney
Secretary.

The learning experience, at Guy's Hospital, though short, was a particularly good one. Additionally, I had two noteworthy experiences there. First, I was selected to be part of the guard of honour for Queen Elizabeth's visit to the hospital. I was thus able to see her from a short distance of about 10 feet. Although I felt honoured to have been selected, I expected her to be taller. The second noteworthy event was that I met and fell in love with one of the medical students. He was a Londoner and, unfortunately, his parents took extraordinarily strong objections to our relationship. We were disappointed and distressed. Once again, I turned to prayer. I was able to see that he needed his parents more, at that time, than he needed me. Even if I could help support him through medical school, he would not have been happy in a battle with his parents who had supported him up to this stage of his life. I decided that it would be better for me to return to Trinidad and Tobago and see what would happen. My plan was to remain there for the foreseeable future. As fate would have it, however, before leaving the UK, a friend, whom I had met during my midwifery training, called and told me that there was a Nursing Director from Canada, in London, recruiting nurses. I decided to go along with her to the interview. I was offered a job in Canada and this turned out to be another blessing. I completed the second part of my midwifery training and returned to Trinidad and Tobago.

Spiritual Growth.

I honestly cannot pin-point any spiritual growth during this time or anytime during my stay in England. I was really on maintenance mode. I tried to attend Mass regularly and pray daily as I was taught as a child. Additionally, the profession which I had embraced, gave me the opportunity to be compassionate, kind and caring. However, I think that my prayers were mainly self- centred, asking the Lord to protect me and help me attain my goals.

Brief Stay in Trinidad and Tobago.

I returned to Trinidad and Tobago as planned, but my life took a different turn. I had thought that I would have no problems obtaining an assignment to work in our own mental hospital, at St Ann's. However, after 3 months of what I considered unnecessary red tape, I decided to take the job in Canada. I think that my ego must have been at work. I was upset, but again I believed that the Lord was in control. I was young and still had a lot of growing and learning to do. I needed an income and salaries in Canada were much higher than in Trinidad and Tobago. My parents were getting older and would need my support, so I went to Canada. I have never regretted making that decision. I did, however, make two other unsuccessful attempts to return to work and live in Trinidad and Tobago during my adult working life.

3

THE JOURNEY CONTINUES: THE GREENER PASTURES, CANADA, 1963 TO 1979.

As a Young Nurse in Canada

3.1: Spiritual Growth

Canada became my second home in 1963. People were friendly and warm, and I made many true lifelong multiracial and multi denominational friends. It was there that I began to grow spiritually, to give of myself and to give back some of what I had so freely received. My first place of residence was Oshawa, Ontario. Oshawa was particularly good to me. It was while I was there that I had my first personal encounter with CHRIST. As mentioned before, I tried never to miss Mass. I remember even running to get to Mass on time when I was a child. I did not understand why, but I got the feeling of happiness every time I went to Mass or to confession and received Holy Communion. I felt renewed and strengthened and I felt that I knew Jesus and that He loved me. Somehow, however, to this point, I believed that He was in Heaven, and this was up in the sky, from where he was looking down on me and sending my guardian angel to take care of me and protect me. However, while in Oshawa, I realized that there was room for a deeper and more personal relationship with Christ, my saviour, brother, and friend. Here, I finally understood what I had learnt in catechism as a child. That is, that God had made me so that I would **Know Him, Love Him and Serve Him.** It happened as follows:

One Sunday evening, I went to Mass because I was on duty that morning. On that fateful day, the priest who was filling in for the parish priest, took notice of me. The next Monday morning, one of the nurses came to me and asked me if I had gone to Mass at Saint Gregory's the previous evening. I told her, "Yes," and she said that Father B, the priest, would like to meet me. He was from a different parish, but had filled in that Sunday. She gave me his number and I called him. He was organizing a "Cursillo in Christianity," the second in Canada. He invited me to become involved, and I agreed.

The Cursillo, or short course in Christianity, is an apostolic movement of the Roman Catholic Church. It was started in Majorca, Spain in 1944, by a group of laymen to find, form, sustain and link Lay Leadership for Christ. Pope St. John Paul 11 described it as follows *"...the Cursillo method aims at helping transform, in a Christian way, the milieus where people live and work through the involvement of 'new men and women' who have become such from their encounter with Christ."* It offers a simple method to seek and develop a Christian spiritually, mentally, and socially, for activity and community. Involvement is not limited to Catholics only. It involves four days. For the first three days, participants live and work together, listening to talks given by priests and laity, as well as sharing the Eucharist and prayers. The three days are intended to bring participants into a closer relationship with Our

Saviour so that we could take Him back home on the fourth day. The "Fourth Day" is the rest of the participant's life. One is expected to live his or her Fourth Day as a continuous time of following in the footsteps of Our Saviour, in loving and serving our fellowmen. One is called a Cursillista after the third day is successfully completed. Cursillistas are expected to become persons in the model stated in 1 Timothy 4:12: *"Be an example for the believers in your speech, your conduct, your love, faith and purity."* Over the three- day weekend, talks are given on Ideals, Grace, Laity, Piety, Study, the Sacraments, Action, Obstacles to Grace, Leadership, Evangelization of the Environment, Christian Life, Christian Community, and Group Reunion.

During my Cursillo, most of the talks were given by the Laity, who seemed as if they were transformed and God himself was speaking to me. On the second day, my heart was touched in an "inexplicable" way and my tears started flowing spontaneously. It was as if my tears were washing me clean. Then, I felt changed. I was never so happy and full of joy. My tears were tears of joy. I emerged from this experience feeling that I knew God in a very personal way! Jesus was not only my Saviour, He was my brother, best friend and confidant. Whereas before I believed that Jesus loved me and died for me, now I KNEW Jesus as my personal Saviour, guide, and best friend, and I felt that I understood the extent of His love. He became really, really, real. I could talk to him at any time, about anything.

Unfortunately, I do not always go to Him or listen to His reply. I have the very human tendency of listening to myself and doing things "my way." This, unfortunately, is not always the best way and I often have to bear the consequences. He lets me have my way, but somehow, He leads me to reflect on my actions and see where I go off track.

At the conclusion of my Weekend, I remember being commissioned to be a "lighted candle." I was reminded that no one "lights a candle and puts it under a bushel." Therefore, I MUST let my light shine. That, to me, meant that I must go out and show my love for the Lord by my life!! I realized then that my Christianity to that point was largely passive or selfish. I always prayed, but mainly it was for God's guidance and blessings for me, or for His help for members of my family or my friends. Sometimes I would reflect and thank Him for His Love, but the focus was mostly on me. The challenge was to become "other focused" and "selfless" in my dealings with others. In other words, I was being called to LOVE.

The Lord had started His grooming as to who I was to become from my childhood, although I did not recognize it at the time. According to family members, I was a warm, friendly, and loving child who was always sharing and smiling. As an adult, the Lord had guided me into a profession where those characteristics of my personality were further developed. I was a caring and compassionate person who enjoyed being a nurse, and whom my patients seemed to love and respect. Several invited me to their homes to meet their families. Two asked me to be godmother to their children.

After my Cursillo, however, I began to realize that the good that I was doing was simply part of my profession and upbringing. I was doing what, to this point, I had been trained to do. I was going to Mass religiously, but I went home after Mass and continued as usual. Whereas there was nothing wrong with that per se, I did not look around me to see if anyone outside of my family, friends, or workplace needed any help. Now, I had to move forward and SERVE, by putting myself third. I had to serve the Lord in a special way through serving others, particularly the poor and the needy, as Jesus did, without counting the cost or looking for a monetary or other human reward. I had to bear fruit, fruit that would last.

The Challenge.

The teachings of that Weekend had to be lived! I promised then that I would serve the Lord with all my heart. The question was, however, "How am I going to do this?" I did not see myself becoming a nun, because to me I was not disciplined enough, and I loved my freedom. Additionally, I looked forward to getting married one day and having children of my own. I also did not see myself as a preacher or evangelist. I asked the Lord for guidance and as I later discerned, all He was asking of me was to follow His example, Serve and Show LOVE to my fellowman wherever I found myself. To do that, however, first, I had to be pruned and groomed, and the skills God had blessed me with thus far, and which I had more or less, taken for granted, had to be pruned, disciplined, and strengthened. I had to recognize and accept that my success thus far was God's gift to me, rather than because I was intellectually gifted or charming in my own right.

My challenge was to reflect on my behaviour, try to gain the grace of humility, perseverance, forthright honesty with myself and others and to radiate love wherever and under whatever circumstances I found myself.

Additionally, I had to be able to discern the voice of God, so I could listen to and follow it, as a prerequisite to doing God's will instead of my own. I had to move from "I, I" and "Me, Me" as the centre of everything to "WE" and "US," whatever is the greater good. Basically, I had to show that I was a Christian by the life that I lived. I was not being called to go out and preach the "Word." I was called to live the "Word," using the skills God had given me and would give me. In this way, others could see my joy, happiness and contentment, and want to emulate me.

I try my best to live out this most challenging commission, and it certainly is not always easy. Challenges and problems have abounded in my personal, professional and spiritual life. I have, however, found consolation and confidence in the knowledge and belief that God knows best and does not make mistakes. Therefore, no matter the challenge, or no matter how far I stray, my brother and friend would be there to help me out, once I turned to Him and asked for His help. I just had to learn to wait for His answer and be prepared to accept whether it was, "Yes, No, or Not Yet."

My "Fourth Day" began with my being invited to join the Leadership Group. I was thus able to share and encourage others in their walk with the Lord. I was assigned the talk on Piety at weekends in Toronto and Montreal.

As A Member of the Women's Cursillo in Toronto, Canada, 1965.

Looking back on my life, I cannot help smiling and remembering my older brother, Basil, who used to tell me, "You have to give to get." I did not think much of his tactics at the time, but I have come to realize that the more I give to others, the more the Lord blesses me. I have become like a funnel or channel, through which He passes blessings on to others, even though I am far from being perfect.

As Team Member at Women's Cursillo in Quebec

We can now look at my blessings: professional, spiritual, and social, and see how closely intertwined they are and why I can honestly say:

"YOU CAN DO THIS AND MORE, YES YOU CAN"

3.2: Professional Growth.

3.2.1: *Mc Gill University, Montreal, PQ.*

A major difference in the education of Nursing students in England and in Canada, in the fifties and early sixties, was that, whereas in England the nursing tutors were mainly in the classrooms, and the head nurses did most of the practical training, in Canada, tutors accompanied students to the wards to supervise their activities, such as doing dressings. When I started work in Canada, I was placed on a surgical ward. After my "Cursillo weekend," although I was not the head nurse, I developed a keen interest in the education of the students. I would invite them to join me whenever I was performing a new procedure. I would also inform the tutors if there was a procedure which I thought the students could benefit from doing. I decided that I liked teaching. It was a career I had contemplated when in high school.

To teach Nursing in Canada, however, meant that I needed a diploma or degree in nursing education. I thus applied to, and was accepted into, a program at McGill University in Montreal. I do not know how word of my plans got to the Director of Nursing. I was, therefore, a little shaken when I was told that the Director wanted to see me. I wondered what I had done wrong and whether I was going to be fired. I was, therefore, greatly relieved and elated when she gave me the reason for the summons. She had heard of my involvement with the students and that I was planning to enter university. She offered me a scholarship! All I had to do was return and teach at the hospital for one year! Without consciously planning it, I had let my "light shine" by reaching out to the students, and this was recognized and was being rewarded. O happy day! Naturally, I accepted the scholarship. I went on to McGill University and obtained a Diploma in Nursing Education.

At Mc Gill, I also met and made some lifelong friends from different parts of the world, as well as other students from Trinidad and Tobago. Studying was hard work, but I enjoyed the university environment as a student. Additionally, my cousin, who had also graduated from McGill as a Medical Doctor, lived in Montreal at the time. He and his family were incredibly supportive and made me feel at home. I was able to bond with his children, who to this day regard me as their aunt. The sojourn in Montreal enabled the strengthening of my professional, social and family life. I continued my attendance at Mass and my contact with other cursillistas. I also started reading the Bible, almost daily. Upon completion of my year of study, I returned to Oshawa General Hospital and fulfilled my obligation.

Back in Oshawa, side by side with performing my job as a teacher, I became more involved with the Cursillo movement. I remained a member of the leadership team and continued to serve in a variety of "Weekends" and "Fourth day" activities in Toronto and in Montreal. At this time, my relationship with my boyfriend from England came to an end. He had completed his medical training and did not wish to come to Canada. I could not see myself living in England. Among other things, I never really liked the English weather. The smog, which covered London in the winter, at that time, was not good for my health and I believed that he knew that. However, over the years we had obviously grown apart. I felt that he must have met someone else, thus the relationship ended. I was disappointed but not distraught. Although I accepted that that was God's will, the whole affair did jade my attitude towards men for a long time.

3.2.2: *University of Windsor, Ontario.*

After fulfilling my obligation in Oshawa, I decided to pursue a Bachelor of Nursing Degree. This I did at the University of Windsor, Ontario. I changed universities because it enabled me to obtain my degree in a shorter time period, by taking courses during the Summer Intercession. Windsor also provided an opportunity for me to test and strengthen my faith. I was there at the height of the Civil Rights challenges in the United States of America (USA). President Kennedy was assassinated when I first arrived in Canada. Now, his brother was assassinated while I was a student in Windsor. I felt hurt, helpless and confused, as did other black students who were at Windsor at the time. However, there was nothing we could do. I remember the event because a number of us spent a good part of the night looking over the river at Detroit, to see if there was going to be a riot. I think we wanted to see some sort of protest. This did not happen, so I prayed for Robert Kennedy's soul and hoped that discrimination would stop. That prayer is yet to be answered.

Racial tensions were high during that time. I had heard of lynchings and other negative occurrences, therefore, as a black person and a foreigner, my first inclination was to avoid the USA. Despite the fact that travelling through the USA as the only black person with a group of four young white women could have been risky, it did not deter me from visiting the USA during the break, as we waited for our summer courses to complete our degree. I was not afraid. I believed that my Lord and friend would protect us.

The trip was enjoyable and added to my educational and social growth. We went through Pennsylvania and saw the Amish people and the way they lived. We then went down to Gettysburg, where part of the American Civil War was fought, visited the museum and the memorial marking Abraham Lincoln's Gettysburg address. We avoided Washington DC because there was to be a great Civil Rights March in that city, and we did not want to get caught in it. We drove to New York to see the Statue of Liberty and the Empire State Building. We headed back to Canada through Boston. Here, we enjoyed the seafood. We got lost a couple of times as there was no GPS at the time. I always remember, with a smile, the day when we could not find our way out of Bethlehem in Pennsylvania and had to be escorted out by the police! They were very helpful. However, the fact that we got lost in Bethlehem struck me as funny. We definitely had nothing in common with the wise men!

Back in Canada, we took a cruise through the Thousand Islands on Lake Ontario off Kingston/ Gananoque and returned to Windsor.

How could a bunch of struggling students afford such a trip? You may well ask. My answer is that it was by being frugal and being humble and willing to share. We were all from different places, including New Zealand, South Africa, British Columbia, Alberta, and of course, Trinidad and Tobago. None of us had ever visited the United States of America. As independent adult workers it could have cost each of us a tidy sum, but as humble students, we decided to share. One member of the group had a car and a credit card for purchasing fuel. We all agreed to share the cost of the purchase. All five of us shared one motel room each night. We occupied a room with two double beds and asked for a cot. We rotated the sleeping on the cot. We took along an immersion heater and a couple of thermos flasks, so we could make and take tea or coffee. We bought items for our breakfast and lunch from the grocery as we went along. We always went to supper. Naturally, we each paid our own way for entry to any event or place of interest. Upon our return to Windsor, we shared the cost for the fuel.

Back in Windsor, the intercession programme went well. I shared a house with a fellow student from St Vincent. Babysitting the owners' dogs while they went for a summer trip to Europe covered our rent. By the end of the summer, I had enough credits to graduate with a Bachelor of Science in Nursing Administration (BScN) Degree.

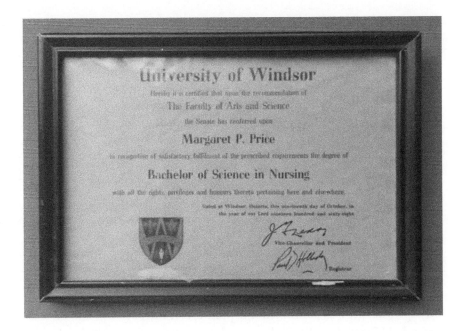

3.2.3: Toronto, Ontario.

Upon graduation from Windsor, I moved on from Oshawa to Toronto as a teacher at the St Joseph's Hospital School of Nursing. There, I was responsible for the Psychiatric Nursing rotation of students. I enjoyed living in Toronto. The population was very multi-cultural and multi-ethnic, and we seemed largely to be comfortable in one another's company. I felt safe since there was not much crime at the time. I could go out to dinner to Chinatown with my friends, go to the O'keefe Centre to plays and concerts, walk down Young street with my friends on any Saturday night, go dancing and have fun.

There was a Trinidad and Tobago (T&T) Association organized by the students at the University of Toronto, to which all T&T nationals were welcomed. I was privileged to join this group and to be involved in the first Caribana Festival. I also met another cousin, a great niece of my father's, for the first time. Although she was born and raised in Trinidad, she recognized my surname and approached me. We were able to establish the relationship and immediately established a close bond.

Celebrating the First Caribana, Toronto.

Spiritual Growth

My spiritual growth continued. I kept in touch with my Cursillo director, attended Ultreas (sharing and spiritual development meetings), and served in the movement in whatever capacity I was called upon. My attendance at Mass became more frequent, as did my reading of the Bible.

I was enjoying life in Toronto and did not visualize a change from there. My cousin and his family had moved to Toronto from Montreal, so I had relatives from both my mother's and father's side there. My father died when I lived in Toronto and I had no problem in bringing my mother to come to visit and spend some time with me. I was very contented with my lot. I had received much more in life than anticipated when I first left my original homeland, and I was very grateful. The Lord, however, had other plans for me. Even though I had become more conscious of my behaviour as a Christian, my grooming continued.

During my stay at St Joseph Hospital School of nursing, there was an advertisement at the School for a Teaching Supervisor. Some of the other teachers thought that I should apply. I am not sure why they did, because I was the most junior in terms of my employment there. I was also one of the only two black teachers on staff. I was flattered, took their advice, and applied, but did not get the job. Whereas I was able to put a positive spin on my failure to get the position, some of the teachers seemed to have been genuinely disappointed. As far as I was concerned, the decision was fine. I believed that the Lord was telling me "Not yet" or "No." The teacher who was successful in obtaining the position had provided years of service to the School and was far more experienced than I was. I was still young. I was grateful to those staff members for their confidence in me and continued to enjoy Toronto.

About a month after being turned down for the supervisor's position, there was an advertisement in one of the newspapers for applicants for the position of Director of Nursing at London Psychiatric Hospital (LPH). I did not see the advertisement, but three fellow teachers and a friend did. Each person addressed me and told me that that was the job for me. I was reluctant to apply. I was 34 years old and simply did not think that I would be given such a position. My sense of humour told me that one had to be "Fair, Fat, and Forty" to get such a position. However, because of my friends' persistence and my firm belief that God speaks to me through others, I applied. Byron Lee and the Dragoneers, a musical band, was coming to Toronto from Jamaica and I was looking forward to going to the event. It was to be on the night before that set for the interview. If I went to the dance, I would be too tired to attend the interview. I was conflicted. I really did not think that I would be successful in obtaining the job, but my friend from Grenada insisted that I forgo going to the dance, and offered to drive me to London. I gave in. In looking back at that event, I realised that I was being pruned once again. I had to give up some of my love of worldly pleasures if I were to move ahead in life.

3.2.4: London, Ontario

3.2.4.1: London Psychiatric Hospital

My job interview was remarkable. As I awaited my turn to be interviewed, I met another nurse who had just been interviewed. She was older, and to me she looked the part for the role of director- "Fair, Fat, and Forty." I asked her how her interview went. She told me that they had asked her what changes she would make if she was given the job. She said that she had told them that nurses needed some "shaping up" and that she had given them a list of what she would do. I thought, "Well that's it; my bad luck, I don't have such a list, and I really have no specific idea of what I would do." I offered her a ride back to Toronto with us and we later became friends.

When I went into the interview, they asked me the same question. "If you get the job what would you change?" I had never worked in a

Psychiatric hospital in Canada, so my response was spontaneous. Being true to myself, I asked them, "What needs changing? How would I know without talking to the staff and finding out what their problems were?" They asked me how I would do that and I told them that I would bring the head nurses and supervisors together for a couple of days, and we would identify, prioritize and discuss the problems, develop a plan, and assign responsibility for getting solutions. They nodded but said nothing. They asked me about the education of students. The answer was easy because I was a teacher and I knew that all students needed experience. They asked me about Unions, and I admitted to not ever having worked with unions, but told them that I was willing to learn. When it got to the fourth member of the four- person interview team, he said that he had no questions. I thought well, that is it. He must have thought that I was wasting their time. They thanked me for coming and said that I would hear from them. I went back to my job without any concern or worry. My consolation was that God would either say," Yes", "No", or "Not yet." I was willing and ready to see this interview as a learning experience and accept whatever decision was taken. After all, I had never worked in a Psychiatric hospital in Canada, and this would be a big leap which I might not be able to make successfully. The summer break was approaching. I had started making plans to go to England and visit family and friends. I had also planned to go on a European tour since I was not able to afford this when I was a student in England. I looked forward to fulfilling this dream.

To my surprise, the next Monday morning, I received a call from the Personnel Officer of the hospital asking me when I could start! I told him that I was planning to go to Europe for the summer and that I could start when I returned. He told me that they had their eye on two of us, and that if I wanted the job I would have to start within a month to six weeks. I accepted the offer.

When I started at the hospital, I found out that I was the only person on whom the team had unanimously agreed. They had gone without a Director for nearly two years! They had two Assistant Directors who had worked at the hospital almost all their working lives but did not choose either of them to fill the post. The Medical Director, the Assistant Medical Director, the Personnel Officer, and the Nursing Tutor from the University of Western Ontario, who constituted the interview team, all felt that they could work with me. I was told that this was because of my honesty, frankness, apparent humility, apparent willingness to listen, to learn and to involve others. I believe that it was a reward for letting my "Light" shine. To me, this was further evidence of my growth as a Christian. I was moving from "I" to "We" and I was Listening. Additionally, I did not have to pretend to be who I was not. I could admit that I did not have all the answers. My parents had taught me that honesty is the best policy, and I thank them for that. Obviously, the Lord had said," YES" this time. I thanked Him and looked for ways to engage in positive actions rather than just give "lip service."

When I arrived on the job, I did what I had promised to do at the interview. I organized regular "Days of Reflection" with my senior staff to enable them to develop and strengthen their problem solving and team building skills. Together, we identified problems, prioritized them and determined ways of solving them. We developed Action Plans and assigned responsibility to the various head nurses and supervisors, either as individual persons or in groups, for their achievement. The model worked. The "Days of Reflection" bore fruit, not only for patients and their level of care, but also for the nurses and supervisors, and for me. Teamwork, management, problem solving, decision-making, communication, supervision, and evaluation skills were identified as weaknesses among the senior staff. With the concurrence of the Medical Director and the Personnel Officer, workshops were organized to strengthen skills in these areas. A Day Care programme for patients who did not really need to be hospitalized on a full-time basis, but who had difficulty fitting back into the community, was successfully instituted. Several other initiatives, including the initiation of a four-day work week, were instituted. This, the staff loved. I reported to the Medical Director daily and obtained his input and support for each initiative taken.

It was clear to me that the supervisors and head nurses knew far more than I did what the problems and the challenges were, and what interventions were most likely to succeed. They all responded positively. They were happy that I gave them that recognition, and as their skills developed they were grateful to me for giving them the opportunity to grow. As for me, I knew that I could not succeed without their high level of involvement. I never felt threatened by their challenges as they grew, rather, I was proud of them. A few decided to follow my example and enter university. I supported them. The senior staff and I continued to have weekly problem-solving meetings. They continued these meetings even after I left the institution, and several of them have kept in touch, even to this day. Whenever I am in London I get together with a group of them to play cards or scrabble and share a meal.

In relation to working with unions, I met regularly with the personnel officer, supervisors and union representatives and tried to understand the role and responsibility of unions. The changes which were being implemented by the management teams were generally supported by the staff, since they were usually involved during the planning stage. The main challenges we faced with the union usually had to do with staff discipline and dismissals. However, whereas before the head nurses were generally reluctant to document unacceptable behaviour, as they became more confident and developed better evaluation skills, they saw the value of thorough documentation and evaluation. They now did this without fear or favour. This reduced the challenge of working with the union.

There was also a Nursing Assistant School at LPH. I now became a Director rather than just a supervisor in the area of Nursing Education, as would have been the case had I obtained the supervisors job at St. Joseph's School of Nursing, my previous place of employment. My previous experience as a teacher enabled me to fulfil this role in a positive way.

With Medical Director, Tutor and Graduating Class of Nursing Assistants

Intellectual Growth

In addition to my obvious growth as a manager, I could see that I needed other skills. One of the problems identified during our weekly staff meetings was that several people who were unable to cope with community life, were using suicidal behaviour as a means of being re-admitted into the hospital. We instituted a Day Care Program where recently discharged patients could come to the hospital on a daily basis, have interaction with others, as well as occupational and recreational therapy. I felt that I needed the skills of an epidemiologist to measure the impact of the interventions that we were making, particularly in the area of suicide prevention. I registered at the University of Western Ontario (UWO) and completed the first year of the Masters in Epidemiology program, on a part time basis. It was then required that I complete the second year on a full-time basis. Because of the high staff rapport, any guilt that I might have felt on leaving the facility to complete the program was minimized. The senior nursing staff, as well as the Medical director, understood my reason for going and were supportive. For my part, I was confident that the staff would be able to continue to grow and to cope. My love had manifested in the respect I was able to show to my subordinates. They felt that love and reciprocated in kind. I knew that I was leaving successors behind.

Spiritual growth

In London, my spiritual growth continued. I went to Mass regularly, asked the Lord for guidance and support and He provided these. I continued to work as a member of a local Cursillo group. We became "friends" of the local John Howard Society, and we drove wives from London to visit their husbands who were incarcerated in prisons in Kingston, approximately 253 miles away. We did this on a regular monthly basis. This enabled wives and loved ones, who could not afford the expenses of a two-day trip, to see their mates. Here again, I felt that I was doing some of what the Lord was asking me to do in Matthew 25: 31-46, and I was happy and contented. It was evident to me that the more I gave of myself and showed love, encouragement and support to others, the more joy, progress and happiness I experienced.

I successfully completed my MSc. in Epidemiology. Unfortunately, I was hospitalized and could not attend my graduation. That hospitalization was, however, a blessing, since it was then that a rare blood dyscrasia was diagnosed. This knowledge has saved my life. It revealed why I was always getting sick after some medications and armed me with the knowledge to inform doctors so that they would know what medications to avoid giving to me. My adviser brought my certificate to me on my hospital bed.

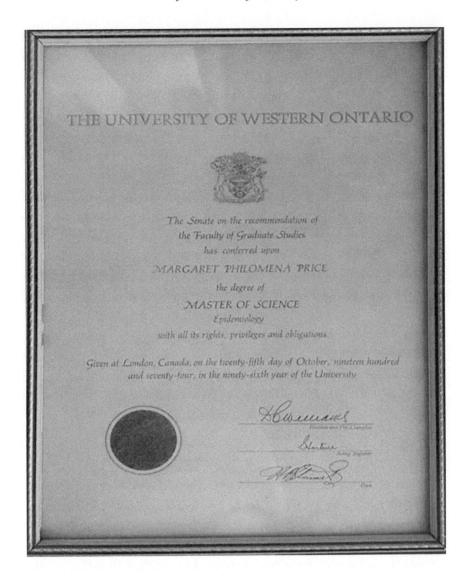

Things take a turn

When I returned from my year's sabbatical with my M.Sc. Degree in Epidemiology, a few things had changed at the LPH. First, the Medical Director with whom I had worked to this point, had retired and was replaced by an Administrator. He was a white American. He seemed to have problems with my colour and style of management. I would describe his style as top down and mine as bottom up. We simply did not see eye to eye on many important matters. I considered him to be condescending. I guess he was trying to make me feel that he was not prejudiced, so he kept comparing me to Diana Ross, the black American singer. Although I liked Diana Ross, I was no entertainer or singer. I was a Senior Manager who deserved to be taken seriously. I certainly did not consider the comparison to be complimentary.

Until this point I had worked with, and had positive relationships with white people throughout my working life and had no interracial problems, at least none that bothered me. I was now in an uncomfortable situation. I must confess that I prayed that he would go away, but I realized that this was not likely to happen because it was a negative prayer done with anger in my heart. Fortunately for me, someone had given me a prayer to the Holy Spirit. It is a prayer in which one prays for enlightenment, guidance, strength and consolation, while earnestly promising to be submissive, humble, and accepting of all that God permits to happen, only that He makes clear what is His will. I started in earnest to seek the intervention of the Holy Spirit. I believe that others must also have been praying for me, because I was able to make a more positive contribution to family and community as I left my problem in the hands of the Lord to show me His will for me.

Social Growth

In addition to working with my local Cursillo group, I started reaching out to others. Moving outside of the family circle, I started befriending overseas students from Africa and the Caribbean. My house was open to them at any time. I listened to their challenges and offered what advice or assistance I could. Some have remained in touch with me in positive relationships to this day. I also befriended other black families, particularly those with children around the same age as my nieces and nephews whom I had assisted to migrate and were then living with me as they completed their education. One of the girls, now a young professional, even assumes the responsibility for getting me from Toronto to London and back when needed. May the Lord continue to bless her.

I sought out and became an active part of the Black community in London. We brought together a chapter of the Black Women's Congress. Here, I was instrumental in organizing an annual fashion show that raised funds to help in the education of poor but brilliant black children. I was viewed as a role model. I am proud to say that one of my nieces whom I had brought to Canada to complete her education, took over this role for some time after my departure from Canada to serve in the Developing world.

For relaxation, personal and professional growth, I was able to attend an international nursing congress in Japan, and visit Hong Kong and Hawaii, as well as British Columbia and Alberta in Western Canada. Additionally, I was also able to make that long awaited trip back to the United Kingdom and Europe.

In Hawaii

Despite my disappointment that I was not able to really apply my new skills as an epidemiologist, I can honestly say, "Thanks be to God," for my experience at LPH. This experience was highly positive in its contribution to my personal, spiritual, professional, social, and emotional growth. It enabled me to develop skills which were to be of great benefit to me and to others who crossed my path, or whose path I crossed. It enabled me to grow in humility. It also strengthened my faith and reliance on the Lord.

As I look back on my life, I can see that it was no accident that I did not realize that I was entering a mental hospital as my first training base in nursing. Had I not received this original experience, I do not think that I would have achieved as much professionally, and maybe spiritually. May God's Will always be done in people's lives.

3.2.4.2: Fanshawe College:

When I first started at LPH as Director of Nursing in 1970, I was invited to and became a member of the Advisory Committee to the Faculty of Health and Welfare at Fanshawe College, the local community college in London. While I was away working on my master's degree, four schools of nursing were moved into the College and there was a need for a Dean. I was not aware of this at the time, but this was to be the answer to my prayer.

A few months after my return to LPH and while I was still concerned about my next step, I was invited to a dinner held by the Board of Directors of Fanshawe College. Seated next to me was the Secretary to the President of the College. As we introduced ourselves to one another at the table, we were each asked to say something about our work life and experience. After I spoke, the secretary said to me, "You are who we have been looking for. You should apply to the president."

I followed her suggestion and I got the job as the Dean of Nursing. I thus became the first Dean of Nursing at Fanshawe College. Once again, the Lord had answered my prayers in a way I could not have imagined. God truly works in mysterious ways. He had answered my positive prayers.

The four Schools of Nursing which were moved into the College were uniquely different, and in many ways competitive. Each School had its own curriculum and personality and they were having difficulty coming together as one. My first challenge was to bring them together with one unified curriculum. Once again, I was blessed. While I was at UWO, I was blessed with having met someone from Wayne State University, Detroit, who was an expert at curriculum development. Although I did not envisage at that time that I would need those skills, I purchased one of her books and we established a positive relationship. I was, therefore, able to invite her to assist me in what could have been a most difficult task. A workshop for the chairmen, coordinators, and supervisors of the four Schools of Nursing was organised and successfully conducted. We repeated this for the tutors, with the chairmen and co-ordinators taking a leading role. Working together, we were able to develop a single curriculum to the satisfaction of all. Subsequently, we started working as one body. Since everyone felt part of what was taking place, the apparent fear of loss of identity disappeared. The rivalry among the various campuses subsided and a feeling of belonging to one body developed. The union representatives were involved in the development process and were supportive of the changes which had to be made.

My First Day as Dean of Nursing, Fanshawe College.

Just over one year after the implementation of the new nursing curriculum, I was approached by the President who offered me the position of Dean of Health Sciences. At the time, there were three health sciences programs at the college, each with its own chairman. The President thought that I could bring them together in the same manner as was done with the nurses. It was obvious that both nursing and the technologies had some common, basic requirements, such as knowledge of basic anatomy and physiology, communication and interpersonal relationship skills. Bringing them together under one umbrella was, therefore, seen as a cost- saving measure. It was possible to align these aspects of the curricula. This was done to the satisfaction of the President, the relevant faculties and the senior management committee. The nursing campuses were, however, still physically scattered and far away from the main Campus. Thus, the full benefit of the potential economies of scale could not be fully realised at that time.

Once again, I was still being groomed. My capabilities were being stretched and strengthened, as were my self-confidence, faith, spiritual and emotional growth. I became a member of the Thames Valley District Health Council; a member of the Sub- Committee on Education of the Co-ordinating Committee of the London Health Council; a member of the Executive Committee, Heads of Health Sciences Programmes, College of Applied Arts and Technology, Ontario, and Chairman of the Western Ontario Region, Heads of Health Sciences programs. Each of these portfolios provided an opportunity for me to grow professionally and become a better person.

I continued to endeavour to walk with the Lord, to read my bible, pray my rosary, listen to God's voice, and serve Him as much as I could.

When the Nursing and other existing Health Sciences programs were working together in a positive and constructive way, I started looking to the future. I felt that there were other health programs which could still be developed at the College. Health Education was one such program. Therefore, when I heard that there was an International Health Education Workshop to be held in Ottawa, I decided to attend. Here again, something life-changing occurred. I met a staff member from the Pan-American Health Organization (PAHO). He told me that PAHO was organizing a training program for tutors in health sciences from the smaller islands of the Caribbean and that they could use my services. These islands were too small for each one to have its own program. I understood and identified with the issue, since I myself was from a small island. The prospect sounded challenging and I had grown to like challenges. However, I was happy and contented where I was. I had attained more than I could have dreamed of when I first left my own "Small Island," and I was enjoying my job and my environment.

I also felt that I would be letting down the President of the College, my staff, and members of the black community, who looked up to me as a role model, should I decide to leave the College. The offer to work with PAHO was on a short-term contract basis with the possibility of renewal. In a way, I was at the top of my professional ladder. I was forty-three years old and I did not actually know what lay ahead. The decision to move from a position of influence and job security to working on a finite contract was, therefore, not an easy one to make. However, here again, based on my firm belief that God talks to me through others, I decided to pray about it, and confer with the President.

After much prayer and reflection, I concluded that there were several people in Canada who could continue with what I was doing or what I had started. I felt that my skills were needed in the Caribbean more than in Canada at that point in time. The President was not completely happy, but he said that he understood why I would think of going to PAHO. He said that the door would be open for me to return to the College at any future date, although he could not guarantee a position. I applied to PAHO and received a two-year contract.

4

INTERNATIONAL EXPERIENCES, 1977 to 1992.

4.1: PAHO (Pan American Health Organization)

The PAHO project was situated in Barbados. I arrived in Barbados and started working as a Health Sciences Educator in September 1977. I was assigned, together with another consultant from England, to prepare Trainers for the Health Sciences Disciplines in the Caribbean. The students came from Grenada, St Vincent, St Lucia, Antigua, Trinidad and Tobago, Guyana, and Jamaica. Included in the group were nurses, public health inspectors, and laboratory technologists. They were highly motivated, and it was very satisfying to see them grow. It was a pleasure working with them. Before the students left to return to their homeland, they had mastered the fundamentals of curriculum development, principles of teaching and learning, problem solving, planning, team building, management and evaluation. The Ministry of Health of Barbados was quite supportive, and provided the opportunity for the students to gain practical experiences.

Moving to Barbados started a whole new growth phase of my life. Not only was I receiving much job satisfaction, but I also felt that I was SERVING the Lord and not just myself. I began to see myself as a "servant leader." All that I had learned before, both intellectually and spiritually, came together in a special way and I felt that I was doing God's will, not mine.

The Cursillo Movement was also in Barbados, so I was able to continue to serve with the group there. I was also moved to join the St Vincent de

Paul Society. This is a society within the Catholic Church that looks after the poor and the needy. It is universal and operates in Catholic churches throughout the world. This provided me with a base from which to serve in many of the countries in which I had the privilege to live and work, after leaving Barbados. It also enabled me to draw others, including the young, to a life of service.

A few activities stand out among my memories of my Service to my fellowman in Barbados. The first was that of having to take an elderly lady to Mass, every Sunday, because her daughter had decided that she no longer believed in God. The second, is that of having to do the grocery shopping for another old lady, my ward. I did her shopping every week because we could not give her the cash, since she had a son who would take the money and buy alcohol. I felt blessed and privileged to be able to serve in this way. I remember this particular old lady because whenever I had to travel and could not do her shopping, and I tried to apologise to her for not being able to do so, she would say, "Don't worry, the Lord understands." That put my mind at ease.

I also befriended a family in which the husband was quite ill. The wife had to work into the evening. Almost every day after work, I was able to replace the regular helper and stay with the sick husband until the wife returned home. I felt blessed to be able to do so. I was sharing Love. After her husband died, the wife and other members of her family became my close friends and I was always able to visit and spend time with them whenever I happened to be in Barbados.

Additionally, in Barbados, I was also able to offer free accommodation and financial help to one student from a sister island. He had lost his scholarship to the university at Cave Hill because he did not perform to the expected level in the first year. I empathized with him because I had experienced problems with studying when I had left my home in Tobago to go to high school in our sister Island. He remained with me and completed his university education. We are still in touch after more than forty years.

In service to the Church, I became a lector and joined the choir. I was also able to work with the youth group. I met and befriended the members of the Madonna House Apostolate, a Catholic community of lay women, lay men, and priest founded by the Russian born Catherine Doherty, in Combermere, Ontario. They live a life of prayer and worship and strive to incarnate the teachings of Jesus Christ by forming a community of love. They are committed to a life of poverty, chastity, obedience, and care of the poor. I was really impressed by what they were doing and was able to work with them, not only in Barbados but later also in Ghana. I was able to visit their Mother House in Combermere, Canada, and added the prayer to Our Lady of Combermere to my repertoire of prayers.

Spiritual Growth

An additional step took place in my spiritual growth while in Barbados. There, I was introduced to the Catholic Charismatic Renewal. The "Life in the Spirit" seminar reinforced and increased my belief and reliance on the Holy Spirit. For the first time, I prayed in "tongues" and experienced spiritual healing. I gained strength to engage in intercessory prayers for others. I realised that it was the Holy spirit who lives in my heart. I found it easier to talk about God and His love to others and to be able to say to others, "God bless you."

Social Growth

On a social level, I was able to make friends, go to the beach every morning, have family and friends come from overseas to enjoy the warmth of the island and its people, take trips around the island, and because of its proximity to Trinidad and Tobago (T&T), I was able to make frequent trips to visit family and friends at home and enjoy our carnival! For what more could I ask? I was incredibly happy and, as usual, I thanked the Lord for His love.

When the PAHO sponsored project was being successfully completed, PAHO started considering the institutionalization of the program, either in the University of the West Indies in Jamaica, or the University of Guyana. I understood the need for this. However, I did not feel that I would be able to really settle in either setting on a long- term basis. I was discouraged by the degree of crime in Jamaica and the politics in Guyana at the time. Once again, I was tempted to try to return and work in Trinidad and Tobago. T&T was planning to start a School of Health Sciences of its own. It seemed to me that I was a good candidate for the position of Director, so I applied. At first, negotiations seemed to be going fine with the then Permanent Secretary (PS) in the Ministry of Health. However, someone whom I trusted and whose brother was a strong supporter of the party in power, managed to undercut me and was assigned the position. I was disappointed and hurt. Once again, I turned to the Lord for help and He answered me with another unimagined blessing.

While I was feeling confused, sorry for myself, and contemplating my next move, a friend, the Health Planner at the Ministry of Health in Barbados, called and informed me that the United States Agency for International Development (USAID), was looking for someone to manage a Health Management Development Project. The project was designed to strengthen the management of the Health systems in the Lesser Developed Countries (LDCs) in the Commonwealth Caribbean and Barbados. The headquarters was to be in the Caribbean Community (CARICOM) Secretariat in Guyana. Once again, I felt certain that the Lord was looking out for me. He was answering my prayers. I was overjoyed and felt more than thankful. I promised to continue to serve God through serving my neighbour. It was obvious that the skills that He was enabling me to develop over the years were now going to be put to the test. I applied and got the job of Project Manager.

As I reflect on my life in Barbados, I realize that life is indeed a journey; that trying to follow Christ and walk in His footsteps is a journey of growth and not a one-time event. In that process of growth, one has to face challenges, tests of ones' faith, the wiles of the devil, as well as ones' innate human nature which predisposes one to sin, and to want to do things, "MY WAY." As a Christian, one must be prepared to grow. Just as Jesus had to overcome challenges to his faith, temptations, persecutions, and threats to his wellbeing, so must we all. The servant can never be greater than the master. When one decides to follow Christ, one should expect to be tested and tried. However, holding on to faith in God, listening to Him and choosing to do His will, bears fruit. We will sin, but He is ever ready to forgive us if we ask for it. I know this for a fact because I am a sinner and despite all my weaknesses, He continues to bless me.

4.2: The Caribbean Community Secretariat (CARICOM)

The job at the CARICOM Secretariat opened a whole new universe for me. The project countries involved included Barbados, Grenada, St

Vincent, St Lucia, Dominica, Antigua, St Kitts/Nevis, Montserrat, and Belize. The project team included an administrator, who was stationed at the project headquarters at the CARICOM Secretariat, in Guyana, a co-ordinator in each participating country and me, as Project Manager. I reported to the head of the Health Desk at the Secretariat. An American company was contracted to provide consultants as required to service the needs of the project. Consultants were hired both from the USA and the Caribbean. The Caribbean consultants came mainly from the University of the West Indies, but also included persons with Health Planning skills from Antigua and Barbados.

Assistance was provided to the respective governments in Health Planning, Management Information Systems, Primary Health Care, the development of Model District Health Teams, and Monitoring and Evaluation. Consultants were contracted to help each national team to develop skills in these areas. The usual procedure was to have the Country Coordinators identify participants, identify and organise appropriate settings for workshops, as well as transportation and accommodation for the training teams. At each workshop, participants were required to develop Action Plans relevant to the area covered and implement them during the next three months. My role as Project Manager included, making final decisions about proposed consultants, determining when and where various programmes would be held, following up to ascertain the level of success achieved with the implementation of the action plans, identifying any barriers to success, determining whether the barriers could be removed, and taking steps to ensure removal if possible.

The countries embraced the project. One Prime Minister insisted that all Permanent Secretaries be part of all training to enable them to develop their management and planning skills. After its conclusion, the UWI, Jamaica, implemented a similar project and invited me to join.

The project enabled me to grow in two significant areas. The first required the development of skills to deal with politicians. Each country had a basic two-party democracy, each with its own unique orientation. I had to learn to work with politicians and/or work in such a way that there was no setback or cancellations of achievements with any change of government. This even involved learning what colour of clothing not to wear in one country.

The project also required my spending a lot of time travelling through the Islands. I did not mind that in the least. However, it also meant that I had considerable time to myself on evenings and weekends during my travels. My per diem enabled me to stay at the best hotels. However, I found their evening entertainment repetitious and after a while, I was bored. I spent a lot of time reading. The students whom I had the privilege of training as tutors when I first arrived in Barbados, and the project coordinators, were excellent in helping me feel at home in each country. I felt loved and blessed. I remember saying to the Lord one morning as I completed my morning swim and was heading to Mass, before going to work, "Lord and I'm also getting paid for this, Thank You."

The second major area of growth led to my becoming a Doctor of Public Administration (DPA). I did a lot of reading related to the content area of the project, but there was a void. I needed to know more about political science and public administration. Once again, a friend was sent to the rescue and I was introduced to the Distance Education Program leading to a Doctorate in Public Administration (DPA) at Nova University in Fort Lauderdale, Florida, USA. This enabled me to focus more intently on Public Administration with an emphasis on Public Health. This was very timely and fitted well into my schedule. The project included Belize and I also found myself working with consultants from UWI, Jamaica. It was, therefore, possible to arrange to be in Fort Lauderdale for the in-house time required for the course, without disrupting my work schedule. It also enabled me to apply the knowledge gained in practical situations in the countries involved in the project. Once again, I was enjoying my work while benefiting professionally.

The time at CARICOM was enlightening and rewarding. I was able to attend Mass and receive Holy communion frequently. I learnt a lot from the consultants who were all highly specialized in their field. In addition to working on my doctorate, I was also able to stop over in Trinidad and Tobago and see my relatives and friends on a regular basis as I connected in my travels up and down the Caribbean. I felt really blessed and could not stop thanking the Lord for this. I felt sure that I had a mission to serve my God by using my skills in the Developing World. I was advising governments! I was working in public health! I was promoting Primary Health Care! Everything was working smoothly. The training I had been privileged to receive thus far was being used in a positive way. At the same time, I was able to give selfless service. I was reflecting my Christianity by the way I was executing the responsibility given to me, and I tried always to give of my best.

The Lord had spoken to me once again through someone else, and even though I myself was not totally sure of my ability in the areas into which I was being moved, I tried to LISTEN, and once again it paid off.

Somehow, there was something about me that inspired others. I remember being asked by two co- workers at CARICOM how I managed to remain so calm and relaxed and always smiling. I shared with them a copy of my prayer to the Holy Spirit. Somewhere along the way, I seem to have lost any tendency to view things in a negative light. The glass is always half full.

During my time at CARICOM, I had my *first verifiable encounter with an angel*. This happened on the Island of St Martin in the Caribbean. One weekend, while working on my Doctorate at Nova University in Ft Lauderdale, I had to travel from Miami to St Kitts to participate in a health planning workshop which I had organised. The route to get to St Kitts was through Puerto Rico and Antigua. When I arrived in Puerto Rico, I was told that since the aeroplane was a small one, my carry-on bag would have to be taken. I handed it over without thinking that it contained most of my funds. I did, however, have some US dollars in my handbag. I thought that I had some extra time before boarding and decided to go to the Duty-free shop and buy a Rubik's Cube as a gift for my secretary's son. I obtained the Rubik's Cube. However, when I approached the boarding gate, I saw the plane taxiing off. Somehow, I did not realise that there was a time change in Puerto Rico that Sunday. I went back to the check-in desk and the clerk informed me that they could get me to St Martin, from whence I could connect to Antigua. I was relieved and boarded the plane.

When I arrived in St Martin, however, I was told that the plane to Antigua had also departed but that there would be one the next morning. I thought that I would have to spend the night sitting at the airport since I now had no funds. The clerk must have seen the look of consternation on my face, so he gave me directions to where the Board of Tourism was located. He was not sure if anyone was there. When I found the location, I met a most beautiful, black lady there. After listening to my problem, she called a hotel and arranged for my accommodation and called a taxi to transport me there and return me to the airport the next morning. She also gave me some money to pay for all the expenses, including the boarding fee for the next morning. I was happy and grateful. I thanked her and told her that I would return the money the next weekend. I asked for and got what I thought was her name and address. The next day I boarded the plane to Antigua where I collected both my regular and carry-on bag.

True to my word, I made plans and returned to St Martin the next weekend. A friend also accompanied me. When we arrived at the airport and the tourist office, I was told that the office was always closed on a Sunday afternoon, and there was no one on the staff by that name or the description that I was giving. Additionally, the address that I had been given did not exist. This was unreal to me. *I knew that I had met the lady I was describing and that the experience I had did occur.* The only logical conclusion I could come to was that *I had met an angel. An angel had come to my rescue.* I was filled with awe at the extent of the Lord's love for me and thanked him. My friend and I enjoyed the weekend and returned to St Kitts, but I was then sure that angels do exist. Maybe my act of love was being rewarded.

Second Return to Tobago

When my contract at CARICOM expired, I decided, for the third time, that I would return to Trinidad and Tobago. I followed my own will and returned to Tobago, my homeland. At first, my stay in Tobago seemed to be going well. I knew that I would need an income, so when I was leaving CARICOM headquarters in Guyana, I decided that I would go into a construction business. I would import Hardwood houses from Guyana, have a team of builders construct them, with me managing the sales. This went well for about one year. I built my own house using the Guyanese hardwood for the upstairs and a concrete apartment downstairs for my widowed sister. I used the upstairs as a demonstration model and several persons bought houses.

I was able to contribute to the community by helping the then chairman of the Tobago House of Assembly to look at programs which could be implemented on the Island. I also joined the St Vincent de Paul Society and the Catholic Charismatic renewal group. I made a group of friends and we got together once a week at my home to say the Rosary. I continued to work on my dissertation to obtain my Doctorate in Public Administration (DPA). Some of my old school friends were still on the island and members of the family seemed happy that I had returned home. I was however, not using the skills which I had been enabled to develop to this point. I really was not fully passing on what was given to me.

By the end of one year, I would say that the honeymoon was over. I LOST A HOUSE! The house was shipped from Guyana and according to the records it arrived in Trinidad. I paid for its clearance, and for its ONWARD shipment to Tobago, but it never arrived in Tobago. I, therefore, had to bear the full cost. I started reflecting on whether I was really supposed to be a businesswoman, whether the Lord was in my decision to return home rather than follow up on the suggestion to go to the UWI. I felt defeated. I felt angry and disappointed in my Country. I had to take a mortgage on my house to cover that loss. For the first time, I wanted to leave and never return. I prayed for guidance. The answer came in two phases and I realised that I was not even half- way through My Journey.

4.3: WHO (World Health Organization)

Towards the end of my stay at CARICOM, I had organised a workshop in Grenada for the development of Management Information Systems (MIS) skills. At that workshop, I had the privilege and pleasure of meeting someone from the World Health Organization (WHO) in Geneva. She was apparently impressed with what was being achieved in the project, particularly in the area of Primary Health care (PHC). When the CARICOM project was completed, she offered me a contract to work with her in supporting the development of Primary Health Care in five countries in Africa. The countries included Zambia, Zimbabwe, Ethiopia, Sudan, and Liberia. Again, my horizon was being broadened. I was learning to apply my skills in cultures, each of which was uniquely different from the western cultures with which I was familiar. I successfully completed that assignment and returned to Tobago. During that assignment, I happened to have met someone from the University of Hawaii, who was also working in International Health. Apparently, he was impressed with my work. He became the vehicle through which I was able to escape from the challenge I was facing in Tobago with the loss of the house.

One day, when I was feeling sorry for myself and thinking that things did not seem to be working out for me in Tobago, and that I was obviously not using the skills that God had given me in a very constructive way, a call came from Charles Drew University's Office of International Health in Washington DC. The Director asked me if I would like to join a team, as the Clinic Management Advisor on a Primary Health Care (PHC) project in Swaziland. The gentleman whom I had met on a previous assignment for WHO, had given her my number and she thought that I would make a valuable member of her team. I told her that she could go ahead and include my name in her proposal. She did, and we won the contract. I was overjoyed to say the least. Once again, the Lord had "come through" for me and I praised and thanked Him.

I had to decide what to do with my house. There was now a mortgage on it, with the land I had inherited from my father as surety. Should I sell it? Should I pay the mortgage from my new income? I was disappointed. I felt sure that I was not ever going to return to live in Tobago. However, after taking it to the Lord, I decided not to sell the house, but I did not want to pay the mortgage either. The choice was to hand it over to a family member or someone who could afford to pay the mortgage. I prayed. I asked the Lord's forgiveness for following my own will, when instead of pursuing the option of going to the University of the West Indies (UWI), I had decided to return to Tobago. Being the loving Father that He is, He gave me a way out of my dilemma.

My mind settled on the nicest young man, my nephew, the son of my best friends. I offered him the house with the mortgage. He agreed to take over the mortgage. His father, my friend, probably read my mind. He did not want me to give up on Tobago. He advised that we should sign an agreement so that for as long as I live, I would retain ownership of the downstairs apartment, the one that I had built for my sister. We did this and my nephew owns the house and I have life ownership of a most beautiful apartment.

I completed my Doctorate in Public Administration (DPA) and headed to Swaziland.

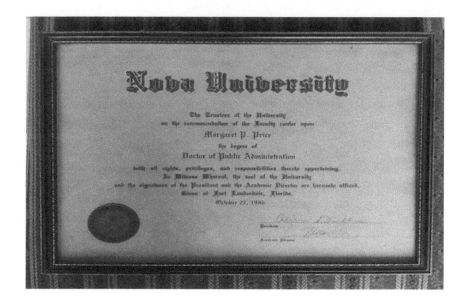

4.4: Charles R. Drew University of Medicine and Science.

4.4.1: Swaziland Primary Health Care Project.

I arrived in Swaziland just after I obtained my DPA. Swaziland is a landlocked, beautiful mountainous country, partially surrounded by South Africa. Many of the native men worked in the mines in South Africa, so many of the families were mainly female headed. I began work as a Clinic Management Advisor. This meant that I had to work in each Region with a team leader and a coordinator. Work went well. I was able to establish and strengthen primary healthcare teams, and to guide the way they worked within the community. I was also able to strengthen the organization and management of the health centres and clinics, and their referral systems. I also conducted workshops to help the Public Health supervisors strengthen their management skills.

At a Workshop on PHC in Swaziland

Workshops were conducted based on the pattern that I had developed in the Caribbean. Community involvement was emphasized. I learnt and respected the national traditions and worked closely with the Chiefs. There was a shortage of Medical Doctors at the community level, and the nurses at the clinics were, therefore, diagnosing and treating clients based on their observations. They had no reference manual to guide them. I was able to collaborate with the Director of Public Health and took the lead in the development of a Clinical Reference Manual for Clinics and Health Centres.

As mentioned before, this went well. When my contract was completed, farewell receptions were held for me. The one done by the Chiefs in the Lubombo region was captured by the press with the heading, "Price Wins Praise for her Priceless Ways." It was not that I was in any way unique, I was just bearing fruits and others were seeing it. I loved what I was doing and was able to show respect for cultural norms and to communicate love in a modest and humble way to others.

In addition to my full-time job as Clinic Management Advisor, I was able to take a leading role in the St. Vincent de Paul society, and in organising fundraising activities to help support the poor and the needy.

I joined the choir and served as a lector from time to time. I befriended a wonderful young man who later died of a ruptured aneurysm. I provided accommodation for his wife and daughter, who was my goddaughter, and accepted responsibility to make sure that his wife was able to get secure employment.

A Misconception Corrected

Before going to Swaziland, I was under the impression that all White South Africans were in favour of Apartheid. While in Swaziland, however, I had experiences which proved the contrary. I also became aware of the stress that those not in favour of Apartheid were undergoing. During a health team meeting at the Northern Region at Pigg's Peak, I met a white South African MD, who oversaw a Roman Catholic Hospital at Emkusweni in that region. He befriended me and invited me to meet his family. I accepted. When I arrived at his home, I was surprised to find that he had adopted a young Siswati child. She was an orphan and her grandfather could not manage her. He had brought her to and abandoned her at the hospital in a severely malnourished state. Dr J. and his wife made the decision to go through all the rigours to adopt her. A black child being adopted by a white South African family! I was surprised.

When I met her, the child had obviously become part of the family and I wondered what would happen to her should they decide to return to South Africa (SA). I could not resist asking him this question. To my surprise, he informed me that he would take the child to live with him, and that she would be able to attend the same Catholic school as his other four children. I was, however, a little sceptical. While I was still in Swaziland, he decided to take the family back to South Africa. They invited me to visit. At that time, apartheid was at its height and there was no way I could have my Canadian passport stamped with a South African visa. I told him that. Again, I was surprised to hear that I could enter South Africa on a visa paper made out to me as an "Honourary white"! I went to the embassy and I was given such a document!

We went to the border and I passed through Immigration on this document! When I arrived in South Africa I was scared. I thought that I would not be able to stay in the all-white neighbourhood where my friends lived. However, I was able to do so. Black people were permitted to visit and work, but not live in those areas. My friends took me to the school, and sure enough, there were black children at the school. I felt immensely proud of my religion. They, my friends, explained that this mixture was permitted by the Church, and other black children could visit them at home. However, their children were not allowed to enter Soweto, the black township in Johannesburg.

A second experience with South Africa had to do with my being invited by an East Indian professor to do some work with the University of Witwatersrand (Vits). Again, I was able to enter SA using the same procedure. The doctor explained the different aspects of the apartheid system specifically as it applied to blacks versus Indians. He took me to Alexandria township, one of the black townships where the University was trying to implement Primary Health Care (PHC). By this time, I was considered a specialist in PHC. What they were doing was interesting and constructive and I was able to make an input. However, once again, I was apprehensive, because the township had only one entry which also served as the exit. I felt that I was in an isolated country within a Country.

I had made other white friends from South Africa, some of whom I had met as a student in England and in Canada. I had also become friendly with some South Africans who had moved their families and residences to Swaziland, while the breadwinner worked in SA during the week. I finally began to understand the strain under which they themselves were living. They loved their Country and would prefer to live there full-time, but were not in favour of apartheid and chose to endure this separation.

During the time I worked in Swaziland, I was also able to visit and holiday in Lesotho, Mozambique, Botswana, Mauritius and Zimbabwe, as well as provide services to a PHC project in Kenya. I was also able to visit, spend holidays and establish close relationships with my nieces in the United Kingdom, and friends in Denmark.

4.4.2: Charles Drew University International Health Institute Washington DC, USA

On completion of my contract in Swaziland, I was employed by Charles Drew University to become their Deputy Director of International Health. The office was loocated in Washington DC although the headquarters of the University was in Los Angeles, California. I was able to enter the US on an H1 Visa. This visa indicated that I was filling a position for which there was currently no qualified American citizen. At that time, (1990), Charles Drew University as a Historical Black College and University (HBCU) was entitled to some preferential considerations for contracts as a minority organization. However, once again politics came into play. The male owners of some of the large international companies objected to this policy. They replaced their names with that of their wives, made the case that women were a minority group, and that they should, therefore, be able to compete against the HBCUs for international projects. These companies were backed by resources that far outstripped the HBCUs. Additionally, they were more experienced and knew how to manipulate the system. It, therefore, became difficult for HBCUs to win contracts on a cost basis.

When I lived and worked in Washington DC, I was able to visit places of interest in the city, Charles Drew University in Los Angeles, Universal Studios Hollywood, Disneyworld, Tijuana in Mexico, as well as family in New York.

Internal changes at Charles Drew University led to the closure of some programs, including the International Health program. Naturally, I was faced with making the decision about whether to remain in the US and move to California, or to return to Canada. Once again, I asked the Lord to intervene and give guidance, and another door opened to me. I was called by a consultancy group who offered me the opportunity to go to Ghana to assist with the development of a training program for traditional midwives. I accepted this obvious blessing, and praised and thanked the Lord. I could swear that my smile got broader.

When I went to Ghana, I not only met some of my grandfather's family, the Quarcoo Family, but once again I met, by coincidence, a gentleman whom I had met five years earlier when I was on contract for the WHO in Geneva. We fell in love and I later moved to Ghana where we were married. I spent the next 24 years of my life there and was able to really SERVE and give of myself.

5

GHANA AND SEVEN COUNTRIES IN EAST, WEST AND SOUTHERN AFRICA.

5.1: Personal and Professional Experiences.

I arrived in Ghana in 1992 at the age of 56 years. My first meaningful activity was to get married. Because my husband and I had each established a reputation in International Health, we agreed that I would retain my maiden name for professional purposes, but his surname in all other circumstances. I was thus henceforth called Dr Margaret Price or Dr (Mrs) Margaret Price Amonoo-Lartson.

When I arrived in Ghana, I had no idea of what work I would do. Once again, the Lord took control and a friend of my husband informed me that the Danish International Development Agency, (DANIDA), was looking for someone to work as a Health Specialist on a Water and Sanitation project that they were planning for the Volta Region of Ghana. I applied and was accepted for the position. The job entailed mobilizing communities to assist in the development and utilization of safe water sources and sanitation facilities. Each district was to have a coordinator who would be responsible for ensuring that planned activities were completed. This included health education on water and sanitation borne diseases, and the benefits of good sanitation and handwashing. Schools and school coordinators, health centres and communities, were all educated along these lines.

Getting persons to change their sources of drinking water was not always an easy task. In some areas, "beneficial spirits" were said to be present in the rivers. Some people, therefore, wanted to continue drinking their river water, even though they were made aware that it was being contaminated in the areas through which the rivers passed, before getting to their village. In addition to community level education, therefore, emphasis was put on the education of the children who were encouraged to advise their parents on the values of safe drinking water.

The project also had to deal with the variety of languages spoken in the region in which it was being conducted. It was necessary to have messages and information translated into different languages. This involved building teams around the language base of the communities they were to serve. Thus, training workshops were conducted. The information was developed in English. The coordinators translated it into their respective language, pre-tested it at the community level, and where there were misunderstandings, corrections were made before the coordinator could pass the information on to the community at large. Ghanaians love to move and dance to music. We, therefore, interjected our messages into popular tunes and this seemed to get the messages to stick.

After three years on the Water and Sanitation project, I decided to pass my contract on to a national who I was sure would do a better job in following up at the community level, since unlike myself, she spoke the local languages. Additionally, I had to be away from home four days per week and this limited the time I was able to spend with my husband, as well as my ability to contribute to my Church community as I would have liked. I returned to my home in Tema.

I established a consultancy firm, the **Health Management Consultancy (HMC) Limited,** and over the years was able to secure contracts from the United States Agency for International Development (USAID), the Canadian International Development Agency (CIDA), the United Nations Children's Fund (UNICEF), the Danish International Development Agency (DANIDA), the United Nations Development Programme (UNDP), the United Nations Population Fund (UNFPA), the Community Water and Sanitation Agency (CWSA), the German Agency for Technical Cooperation (GTZ), and the World Health Organization (WHO), among others. Later, when HIV started ravaging Africa, I was able to help in the development of proposals to obtain assistance from the Global Fund, through UNAIDS, first in Ghana, then in Sierra Leone, the Gambia, Kenya, Nigeria, Southern Sudan and Mozambique. I was also contracted to assist in the development of its proposal by the Government of Barbados, West Indies.

A Training of Trainers manual in Community-based Home Care for persons living with HIV/ AIDS was developed and trainers were trained, in collaboration with the Christian Health Association of Ghana, (CHAG), and UNAIDS. A Water and Sanitation manual for teachers of health education in schools was also developed and school supervisors in the Volta region were trained in its use. I had the opportunity to work in each of the then ten regions in Ghana. Areas of involvement included, Program development, Evaluation, Training of Trainers, the development of Psycho-social Life skills related to the areas of Water and Sanitation and HIV/AIDS. I was also contracted to work in Nigeria and Kenya, courtesy of the World Bank. All these activities were intertwined with my service to my maker.

In the early 1990s, computers were just being introduced and skills in this area needed to be developed. I established a computer training school and was able to provide employment for ten (10) persons and training, free of charge, to some persons who needed these skills but were unable to pay for them. One member of this latter group turned out to be a computer genius and now provides computer training and the development of networks in other countries in Africa.

Conducting Workshops in Kenya and Nigeria

5.2: Spiritual Growth and Service

When I first arrived in Ghana, I asked my future husband to take me to a Roman Catholic Church. He told me that there were three churches in the area and decided to take me to see them. He started by taking me to the Good Shepherd Parish (GSP). As I entered that church, I felt certain that I had finally arrived at the base from which I was to serve and use all those graces and spiritual gifts that God had been developing in me over the years. I knelt and recommitted myself to Him. I declined the offer to be taken to see the other Churches since that was not necessary. I had found where I was supposed to be. It was. For the next 24years, being a member of the Good Shepherd parish fed my spiritual growth. It was here that I saw my call to be a "Servant Leader" really bearing fruit.

Standing Besides a Statue of The Good Shepherd

5.2.1: The St Vincent de Paul Society

On the first Saturday morning when I attended Mass, I was approached by a parishioner who invited me to join the SVP Society. I smiled and thanked her and told her that I had been a Vincentian (member of the SVP society) for years, was glad that there was a SVP society in the Parish, and that I would be happy to join. I joined and found new brothers and sisters. I remained a member of the Society for the entire time during which I lived in Ghana. I became the President for many years, started Conferences in four outstations when I became Chairman of the Outstations Committee, and initiated two groups of junior Vincentians, one at the GSP and another at the Holy Family Parish when I had cause to move there to help my three adopted granddaughters to settle, upon the untimely death of both of their parents.

Over my twenty- four- year residency in Ghana, I was able to serve individual persons and communities in ways that I hoped would not only help them meet their physical, but also their educational and spiritual needs. I was enabled to do this through my Parish Church.

5.2.2: The Missionaries of Charity

One of my first outreach activities in Ghana was to the Missionaries of Charity. I did not know that these missionaries were in Ghana, but one day I went to the sister Church of St Joseph the Worker to see how I could help. I was taken by the Parish Priest to meet the Sister in charge of the group. I was told that they had been given a piece of land on which they were planning to build a Convent, but the land was covered with thorns and that they needed to have it cleaned so that the builders could start construction work. I told her that I would see what I could do. As usual, I took it to the Lord and an answer came to me. "Why not ask some of the youth at the Parish to help?" This sounded good, so the next Saturday morning after Mass, I asked the young man who was the senior member of the "Mass Servers" for help. He was fantastic. The first week he brought me nine young men, the number grew and within a month I had fifteen (15) helpers.

My husband let me use his Pajero and every Saturday morning, after Mass, we spent two hours cleaning the land. These young men were extremely happy to help. I remember one day the rain started falling, and I tried to get them to take shelter. They ignored me and started singing, "There shall be showers of Blessing." The land was cleaned within a month and construction was able to begin. The group continued to work on the site, planting fruit trees and keeping the area clean. They had adopted the Sisters. Together we kept in close contact with the Missionaries of Charity Sisters and I was asked to go to Rome as a friend, at the beatification of Mother Teresa. I continued working with the Sisters as they opened the convent. When HIV/AIDS treatment became available, I took HIV positive residents from the convent to the treatment facility in Accra. I was also able to set up a support system for those who responded positively to treatment.

Kissing of a Relic of St. MotherTeresa and Receiving a gift of Gratitude

5.2.3: My Children

After a while, I realised that the group of young men who were working with me in helping the Sisters, was performing the services of Vincentians. I asked them if they wanted to become Vincentians. They said, "Yes," and the Junior Vincentian Conference was formed, the first in Tema. It is remarkable that the 2Nd and 3rd Presidents of this group of juniors went on to become Priests. A third member who could not get into the priesthood decided to leave the RC Church and join a Pentecostal group, where he is now a Pastor. All but three of the other boys completed their secondary education and education to university level. I was blessed with having the ability to assist them to advance educationally as much as possible. Many seem to be following my example in reaching out to others. My husband passed in 1996 after only four years of our marriage. I contemplated returning to the West where I had biological family and old friends. I thank God that these young men, who had somehow become my sons, convinced me to remain in Ghana.

I was also blessed with the opportunity of being surrogate mother to five girls. The first was my goddaughter whom, my sister asked her family to allow to live with me upon my husband's death. They agreed and that led to my becoming a member of their family. The second was an orphan. The other three needed my help and came to live in my home. The first two have obtained MA degrees, one is moving towards getting her doctorate; one became a caterer, one a fashion designer, and one a Pharmacy Assistant. I am very proud of them, and I pray that the Lord would give them the grace of perseverance in faith. All they needed to help them grow was respect, encouragement, and support given with LOVE.

I also acquired three granddaughters for whom I am responsible. They are three sisters who, when between the ages of 5 and 8 years, came into my room one morning and asked me if I would be their grandmother. Their second grandmother had just died, and the parents had left them with me as they travelled to the village for the funeral. I said, "Yes," without thinking that I would later have to seriously fulfil the role of grandmother, as they became orphans at an early age, when the last two had not completed their education, and the eldest had not yet completed her national service. As I write this, my second granddaughter has now graduated with a BA degree and the third is well on the way to fulfilling her dream of becoming a medical doctor.

I thank the Lord for opening my heart to loving others outside of my biological family in such a deeply personal way. To me this is one of the best fruits that I was able to bear in actually serving the Lord and doing His will and not mine. It is an understatement to say that I feel blessed and Highly favoured.

Sons, one of my Daughters and First Group of Junior Vincentians

5.2.4: Housing a Basic Christian Community

Soon after my bereavement, the Parish started the Renew Program. I was made a leader and my home also became the hub of one of the Basic Christian Community (BCC) Cells. This meant that other Catholics in the neighbourhood met at my home every Monday night to read and discuss the next Sunday's readings and, occasionally to participate in Holy Mass.

There were twenty-three (23) BCC cells in the Parish. Another parishioner and I were identified as leaders with the added responsibility of ensuring that each Cell was meeting and operating according to protocol. The BCCs provided remarkable opportunity for growth. Whereas before I had only the message that I received from the readings, and/or that given by the priest at Mass, I now had the benefit of messages and insights from a larger group of believers. Additionally, we became a Community, sharing problems, joys, and concerns, and helping meet one another's needs. As a result of this, I became the mother of an additional 2 daughters, one whose parents had both died within a nine month period and one who obviously had superior abilities, but who was from a very large family which was not able to ensure her education. I acquired a fourth daughter from my work in the outstations and a fifth from my work with Persons Living with HIV/AIDS. These all ended up living at my home and now operate as sisters looking out for one another's interest.

My house became a house of prayer, with one room as a Prayer Room where we gathered to pray daily as my mother had done with us her children. Over time, I also had three young men sharing my home. They see themselves as my sons. Thus, although I was never blessed with giving birth to any children of my own, I now proudly say I have twenty (20) children! They not only call me, "Mum," or, "Ma Mere," as one of them chooses to do, but relate to me as their mother and to one another as siblings. What is most reassuring to me is that they all love the Lord. Additionally, when I returned to Ghana three years after I left to return to the West, I found out that they had established a platform called, " Sons of Price," and were keeping in touch and sharing important aspects of their lives with one another. I feel extremely blessed as they keep in touch and show concern for me as I grow older.

5.2.5: Consecration of my Home to The Sacred Heart of Jesus.

When the Sacred Heart Confraternity was initiated in the Good Shepherd Parish, I became a member. In addition to having a Prayer Room, I decided to consecrate my home to the Sacred Heart of Jesus. The ceremony was performed by four priests. Two of them Salesians with whom I was working in a neighbouring community. One was from the Madonna House Apostolate with which I had become involved since my stay in Barbados, and one Diocesan, who was a member of my BCC Cell while doing his pastorals before his ordination.

As a member of the Sacred Heart Confraternity, I started making regular weekly Adoration of the Blessed Sacrament, novenas with the group, and saying the Divine Mercy prayers. These all contributed to the strengthening of my faith, thereby making it easier for me to serve. As I grew spiritually, I was able to take leadership roles in societies taking care of children, the aged, the poor, prisoners and the sick. I was also willing and able to help the needy, especially the young in ways that could help them to grow spiritually, socially, educationally, and emotionally. More importantly, I sought opportunities for selfless giving, namely giving without getting any material benefit or return. Matthew 25:31-46 became my reference point. I live in hope of being among the Sheep at the final judgement.

Consecration of my Home to the Sacred Heart of Jesus

5.2.6: Vice Chairperson of the Parish Pastoral Council

Because of my work and interest in the environment, I became a formative member of the "Women's Action Group on the Environment" at the Parish. In addition to accepting responsibility for the maintenance of the physical environment of the parish, once a year we planted trees around the Parish and joined the broader Archdiocesan group in supporting tree planting in specified areas in the Greater Accra region. The members of this group nominated me to represent them on the Parish Pastoral Council. At the Council meeting, I was selected as the Vice Chairperson, and because of my then involvement with some of the outstations, an outstations committee was formed, and I was made the Chairperson.

5.2.7: Chairperson of the Outstations Committee.

As Chairperson of the Outstations Committee, I led in the development of many poverty alleviation projects in the related communities. Among these were the development of a mango plantation, the establishment of a Gari Processing Centre for widows, a school- feeding program for orphans, and the beginning of the re-building of a dam so that fish farming could be done while water can be controlled to enable year-round farming at the lower end. I really began to see the living Christ in others, and as I said before, I became more alive, happier, more joyful and fulfilled.

My involvement with the outstations was initiated by the then Archbishop who was interested in the development of one community. He felt that I could work with his Development Officer to identify the needs of that community and recommend necessary interventions. We did that, and in consultation with the community decided that the starting point for intervention was a partially completed dam which, if properly completed, could contribute to fish farming and to down-stream agriculture. With financial support from Ireland, the project was partially completed when the Development Officer died. The new Parish Priest, Rev. Fr. C, took over and completed the project.

The original assessment had revealed many unmet needs. There was a high degree of unemployment and poverty in that village. Additionally, many children were being raised by grandparents, either because their parents had died or had moved away. The grandparents were poor and could not afford to send them to school. I was able to raise funds to buy uniforms as well as support for a cook and food from the World Food Program to prepare school meals. This motivated the grandparents to send the children to school since they were receiving two meals daily. The program was later taken over by the then in-coming government.

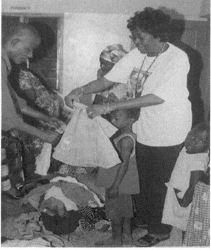

Some Beneficiaries of the School Feeding Programme and Young Orphans

In addition to the School Feeding Program, there was a used clothing outreach to children. This was also appreciated by the community. The poverty of the grandmothers, however, still had to be addressed. As Chairperson of the Outstations Committee, my team and I undertook many initiatives to address the poverty situation as far as we could. This included the establishment of a Gari Processing Plant for the grandmothers in the village, as well as the development of a six acre mango plantation from which the newly established SVP society was to obtain funds to help in supporting the orphans with their education.

Gari Makers

We procured and supplied used clothing to adults from time to time. During this period, I realised that there are many people around who want to serve and give of themselves and would do so if given the right leadership and encouragement.

The Outstation Committee was also instrumental in assisting with the final preparation of a community clinic building and in helping the Holy Family Sisters, who were to be responsible for the Clinic, to settle in. We also supported the construction of durable church buildings in three other outstation communities under the supervision of the Parish Priest. We planted another six-acre farm with cashews in another Community. This, unfortunately, was destroyed by fire that was set by cattle herders.

5.2.8: Justice and Peace Commissioner.

One fine day, my Parish Priest informed me that he had just come from a Deanery meeting of priests at which I was nominated to be the Deanery representative on the Archdiocesan Justice and Peace (J&P) Commission. The nomination was made by a Selesian priest from another community in which I helped with a Street Children Program from time to time. Each of the ten (10)

Archdiocese in the Country at that time had a team made up of representatives from its deanery. Our role was to explore and address issues of Justice and Peace at the three levels, and inform the Catholic Bishop's Conference where their intervention was necessary. We also had the responsibility of facilitating the formation of Parish level Justice and Peace Committees, and preparing and supervising election observers in our districts.

As a Member of the Archdiocesan Justice and Peace Commission

5.2.9: *Extraordinary Minister of the Eucharist*

In 2004, I was appointed an Extraordinary Minister of the Eucharist.

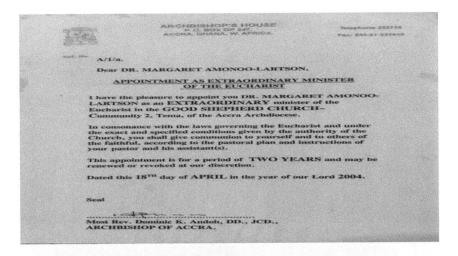

With Parish and Associate Priests and Fellow Ministers.

5.2.10: *Mother of the Year*

In 2006 I was Selected and Honoured as Mother of the Year.

Mother of the Year

5.2.11: A Day Care Centre for the Aged.

Through the leadership of the parish priest of the GSP, the SVP Society of the Tema/Battor Deanery was given a parcel of land on which to construct a Day Care Centre for the Aged. My final major contribution to my brothers and sisters in Ghana was the leadership provided in bringing this Centre to a reality. I was able to provide leadership in fund raising, supervision of the construction, development and implementation of the program of activities, involvement of the leadership of other denominations in the area, and involvement of the industries and companies in Tema, to assist with the provision of furniture and other essentials, such as foodstuff on a regular basis to sustain the program. Additionally, I was able to persuade a group of medical doctors and a pharmacist, who had empathy for the aged, to provide regular monthly clinical services at the centre, to the aged in the area.

6

RETURN TO THE WEST/Reflections

At one point, life in Ghana seemed to be getting stressful. I was having problems getting reliable workmen to take care of the lawn, cut the hedge, clean the pool, and watch the house at nights. The children had all grown and were starting to live their own productive lives. I felt that the house/ property on which I lived was too large for me alone at that stage and that it was time to downsize. Additionally, I was feeling a little sorry for myself. I felt that I was not getting the necessary support from the Deanery section of the SVP Society to run the Home for the Aged. My stamina was getting low. I felt that my life could soon be coming to an end, since I had been a diabetic with hypertension and a blood dyscrasia for almost thirty (30) years. Then came a strong desire to spend my last days with my biological family. As time went by, I had grown out of my negative feelings about the loss of that house in Tobago and began to see it as a blessing, even though I cannot honestly say that it was easy for me to forgive that person or persons who hijacked it. At age eighty, therefore, I decided to return to the West and spend my remaining days between Canada and Tobago.

I spoke to my spiritual advisor. He saw Ghana as my home and suggested that I go for a holiday and think things over. My mind was, however, set on getting back to the West. One morning, I woke with an extremely clear message that I should read and reflect on the Books of Ephesians, Philippians, and Colossians. I had to reflect on them before making a final decision. I read them and it was as if the Lord was challenging me regarding the fulfilment of my mission in Ghana. I had never even thought about having a mission. I wrote my reflections down as they came. I share these with you as they came to me.

6.1: Reflections on Reading the Book of Ephesians

Today, I came to the full realization of how much God loves me. I completed reading the letter of St. Paul to the Ephesians and although I had read and heard the words before and had tried to be guided by them, God brought the memory of my mother to my mind and I reflected on how much she loved me. How she would correct me, chastise me, and encourage me to pray. Yet, despite my failures and shortcomings, she never gave up on me. Here, God was telling me that even though my mother and father may forsake me, He would never forsake me, therefore, whatever my final decision He would be there.

Going forward my responsibilities are to:

1. Be faithful to the Lord Jesus Christ.
2. Try to be holy and blameless in love.
3. Believe that I am sealed in Christ, the truth, and sealed with the Holy Spirit of Promise.
4. Pray for a spirit of wisdom and revelation in the knowledge of Jesus Christ.
5. Live in a manner worthy of my calling, with humility, gentleness, patience, showing tolerance for others in love, being diligent to preserve the unity of the Spirit and the bond of peace as prescribed in Ephesians 4:1-3.
6. Remember that grace is a gift from God to be whatever He ordained, evangelists, teachers, prophets, to equip us to serve.
7. Not be tossed about by various waves/ doctrines but to speak the truth in love, to grow in all aspects into Christ who is the head.
8. Put on a new self in the likeness of God in righteousness, holiness, and truth.
9. Be angry but do not sin. Do not let the sun go down on my anger.
10. Watch my speech. Speak only for edification- to give grace to those who hear.
11. Put away all anger, bitterness, wrath and slander. DO NOT GRIEVE THE HOLY SPIRIT.
12. Try to be an imitation of Christ.
13. Give thanks always.

14. Walk in the light. Try to lean towards what is pleasing to God and to do His will. Fear the Lord.
15. Be on guard always.
16. Not be an eye servant
17. Put on the full armour of God, so as to be able to stand firm against the schemes of the devil. Take righteousness as a breastplate, faith as a shield, the helmet of salvation, and the sword which is the word of God.
18. Pray at all times in the spirit; persevere and petition for all God's chosen (the saints).
19. Be bold in proclaiming God's word.

As I reflected on this book, I realized that as much as I might have tried, I could have fallen short in many areas. Thus, I still had some growing to do. My question was, "Do I have to stay in Ghana to do so?" I began to ask myself, "Am I removing my hand from the plough?" I however, told myself that I could fulfil all of the above where ever I found myself if I remained committed to my role as servant. I proceeded to re-read the letter to the Philippians.

6.2: Reflections on Philippians

I was experiencing a sense of failure. I felt that I had fallen away from my close relationship with Christ which I had enthusiastically embraced at Cursillo in 1965, and which strengthened me to put the love of God and love of neighbour ahead of all else. The fact that I recently lied to protect a friend whom I thought was going to be unfairly ostracized, even though I knew that that lie would hurt another friend, a priest, had until then haunted me. Although I had apologized and the priest had said that he had forgiven me I still felt guilty. I had difficulty forgiving myself. Additionally, the fact that I was succumbing to pressure from adversaries and was walking away from a project meant to help persons living with HIV, the poor and aged, just compounded my sense of failure. This reading led me to realize that the good Lord had not given up on me. As He said in Philippians 1:6, "He who began a good work in you (me), will perfect it until the day of Jesus Christ."

I was brought to accept the fact that, as a Christian, I am going to have problems and conflicts, but that these would turn out for the greater spread of the gospel and the glory of God, if only I would continue to:

- Proclaim Jesus Christ as my Lord and saviour, to the glory of God the father.
- Stand firm in the Spirit.
- Conduct myself in a manner worthy of the Gospel of Christ.
- Accept that opposition is an integral expectation when I am serving the Lord, that it has been granted for Christ's sake, not only to believe in Him but also suffer for his sake.
- Remember that whether I live or die, I belong to Jesus Christ, and to die for him would be gain.
- Do nothing from selfishness, or empty conceit, but with humility of mind, always regarding others as more important than myself.
- Do not merely look out for my own personal interest but also the interest of others.
- Always remember that Jesus, although the son of God, humbled himself to become a man, did not claim equality with God, but humbled himself and died for my sins.
- Do all things without grumbling or disputing.
- Rejoice in the Lord always.
- Beware of the evil one and be always on guard.
- Work constantly to attain perfection in Christ. I am a work in progress.
- Forget my past sins and reach forward to what lies ahead, the prize, the upward call of God in Christ Jesus.
- Do not set my mind on earthly things.
- Stand firm in the Lord.
- Be anxious about nothing, but in everything with prayer and supplication, with thanksgiving, make my request known to God. (Philippians 4:6)
- Dwell on things that are true, honourable, right, pure, lovely or of good repute, and anything worthy of praise.
- Remember I CAN DO ALL THINGS THROUGH CHRIST WHO STRENGTHENS ME. (Phil 4:13) So, take everything to

the Lord to obtain His blessings, strength, and approval and then do His will, and God will supply all my needs according to His riches in glory in the Lord Jesus Christ.

I, therefore, felt reassured that I am a work in progress. I was getting guidance, but I still had the third book, Colossians, to read and reflect on.

6.3: Reflections on Colossians

In reflecting on the book of Colossians, I came to the realization that it was "OK" for me to slow down, to concentrate not so much on "Doing" but on "Being." At the age of 80 years, my life should be one of gratitude to God:

- Always giving thanks for everything whether it seems good or bad. The Lord is in control. Being faithful; walk in a way pleasing to God, bear fruit and strive to increase my knowledge of God.
- Being patient and joyful, remembering that Jesus died to reconcile me to God despite my sinfulness. He is my hope of Glory.
- Proclaiming Him always in my thoughts, words and deeds, by His grace, and walking in His ways.
- Being always on guard against the guile of the evil one. Remembering that I have been circumcised (made holy) by Christ.
- Remembering always that I died in Christ, and that He, having forgiven all my sins and transgressions, having nailed them to the cross, made me alive together with Him.
- Now, I must put on the new self and keep seeking things above where Christ is seated at the right hand of God.

After reading the three books, I felt that I was being freed to leave Ghana, but that my "Being" was to become a key focus. I felt the need to assess the impact of my commitment to Service and my Being to this point. Did what I had been doing make any lasting impact, and if yes, in what way? What is my legacy?

7

LEGACY

As you would recall, when I outlined what I felt I was being asked to do with my life at the Cursillo weekend, I said that I understood that I was to serve and to live my life in such a way as to be an example to others so that they would want to emulate me. At age 83 years, the question I now asked myself was, "Have I done that? What examples have I left or am I leaving behind?" To answer this question, I had to look to others and ask them a few basic questions to see what impression my life had made on them, beyond the fact that I might have helped them achieve their goals. I, therefore, requested a few of those whom I considered to be my sons and daughters, members from my late husband's family, and a few friends and acquaintances with whom I had worked, to give honest feedback to the following six questions:

1. Describe me as you see me.
2. What, if anything, attracted you to me when we first met?
3. Have I influenced your life in anyway?
4. Has your life or world-view changed in anyway because of me, and how?
5. What do you particularly like about me? (This is not a eulogy.)
6. What do you particularly dislike about me? Don't be afraid to say. It could help me change for the better and I will not love you less.

I decided to group the answers to each question of the first six responders together, with the initials of each respondent and the following code by which they could be identified. For example: S= Son; D= Daughter; WM= Workmate; HF=Husband's Family, and Ad.FM= Adopted Extended Family.

Answers were as follows:

1: Describe me as you see me.

- A mother for all, a person who makes herself available to everyone with whom she comes into contact. (R.S- *Ad. FM*)
- You are a very kind, loving, spiritual, and God-fearing person. You are resourceful and solutions oriented. Family means all the world to you and you are blessed by God. (A.L-*HF*)
- You are a free- spirited, selfless Christian (M--*AD*)
- A mother God gave me in place of my biological mother. Aunty Margaret! You have gone all lengths for me. You love me unconditionally and each step of my life since our first encounter has been love, bringing me close to God and devotion to him and giving me an education. (M.A-*AD*)
- Auntie Margaret is a great woman of faith whom I believe committed her life to the betterment of her friends, family and any community in which she found herself. I was dazzled when after interacting with her for a few minutes, she looked at me and said, " I doubt that you know that you are a young woman with so much greatness ahead of her."(RDS- *AD*)
- You are a very humble and kind person who is always willing to give of herself to others. (LD-*WM*)

2. What, if anything attracted you to me when we first met?

- When we first met it was because you heard my last name and you were curious, not just curious, but you drew me closer to you and to my quiet, late uncle, who was "closed" like my dad. I saw an uncommon genuineness, also authenticity, and openness in you, which I still don't find around. Over time, I felt your presence in the greater Lartson family, as one to shake our coldness and introduce warmth, and help to bind us together (A.L- *HF*)
- Your sense of service to God and mankind, humility, selfless nature to people. (RS—*Ad.FM)*
- Your unconditional love for everyone. (M *A.D)*

- It was the Basic Christian Community meeting that you were hosting in your home and I would come with my Mum and siblings. From there, I could see the pure love, care, intelligence and your accomplishments, and I always admired you. (M.A- *A.D*)
- Auntie Margaret took me into her home with open arms even though she had never met me before, and the year I spent with her prepared me up for the next chapters of my life. Her resilience, strong character, and relationship with her community, and her educational background, had a great impact on me. (R.D.S-AD)
- You were doing what I was aspiring to do in my career, namely public health on an international level. You had accomplished so much in that field and that was noticeable. Oh, the other thing that attracted me to you was that you were from the Caribbean, like me!! (L.D- WM.)

3. Have I influenced your life in anyway?

- Absolutely, absolutely, I feel more connected to the greater Lartson family; you were a part of my journey to the US; you made my nuclear family loving. I once published a book, thanks to you. You will do anything in your power to help me. (AL-HF)
- Yes, yes, yes. Any time I see you I have a sense of how to serve God because you showed me the way to do it. (RS-Ad FM)
- Of course, to love everyone despite his or her background and denomination. (M -AD)
- Yes! Yes! Yes! To be better. To love. To serve God, to give, to never give up, and excel. (M.A- A.D)
- Auntie Margaret helped change my perspective on life. I stopped putting myself down and today, with all humility and appreciation to God and my darling Aunty Margaret, I have been able to commit myself to and complete various life projects. **(RDS-A.D)**
- You were a role model to me who made me know that I could achieve the career dream I had, as a black person in a very closed, white dominated field of work, namely, international health. It was your influence that got me the two-year visiting scholar assignment at CDC. They really wanted you to be in that role,

but you had other plans and you skilfully engineered me into the position. That was a major turning point in my career and life. (L.D-WM)

4. Has your life or world view changed in any way because of me and how?

- I see the world in a number of lenses because of who you are and how you've touched me. (A.L-H.F)
- Yes. You showed me that no matter a person's nationality, tribe, or whatever, all people are the same. (RS-Ad.FM)
- Yes... having empathy for one another (M—A.D)
- Yes! My faith and trust in God and I am a better person now because of you (M.A.- AD.)
- Because of your deep devotion to God as a Catholic, I gained a different view of Catholic believers. I attended Catholic high school in Jamaica and came away with a really jaded view based on what I saw from the nuns. Furthermore, they never mentioned the relevance of the Gospel to me personally, so I didn't understand the availability of salvation, and that was really sad. Going to Mass with you in Ghana gave me a view of Catholics that I had not experienced before. It was authentic and eye-opening. (L.D- WM)

5. What do you particularly like about me? (This is not a eulogy.)

- How much you have done for others you did not know, and who otherwise might have different lifestyles, possible perhaps terrible lives. This is a manifestation of your love for humankind. (A.L-H.F)
- You are a mother, a friend, a good person. You care. (R.S-Ad FM)
- Your love for the things of God and your support of all those you meet. (M-AD)
- You are an inspiration to me in all aspects of my life. Thank God, our path crossed for you are my Angel. (M.A-AD)
- Auntie Margaret is a selfless woman of God. She has shaped several lives that ordinarily could have been wasted. I am thankful

for the gift of Auntie Margaret in my life. Her faith and approach to life are commendable and worthy of emulation. (RDS-AD.)

- You also influenced me on a personal level through your marriage in your fifties. Again, you served as a role model for me in that way. It was, therefore, an honour to be at your wedding, and serve as your maid of honour. What do I like about you? Lol!! 😄 You have a carefree, confident, gentle spirit and attitude about life. You are unstoppable and whatever you put your mind and hands to, gets done. You find ways around obstacles. You are wise. (L.D.-WM)

6. What do you particularly dislike about me? Don't be afraid to say, it could help me change for the better and I will not love you less.

- Not a dislike but a vulnerability. Like me, you trust people easily. However, unlike me, you keep them even after they disappoint. Love you Auntie Margaret! (A.L-HF)
- Funny question. Not anything in particular. Perhaps your quest to get things done properly and the pressure that comes with it. Ha, ha, ha. Just kidding, truly. (RS-Ad FM)
- It was way back when I used to clean thoroughly but u would still return and tell me I did not do it well 😩....but you were just helping me. (M- AD)
- Aunty Margaret, you are just selfless, regardless.(M.A-AD)
- Thank you, Auntie Margaret, for all you do. Thank you for allowing God to use you positively in the lives of everyone around you. (RDS-AD)
- Can't think of anything really. Can't recall any disagreements we had in the past. We seemed to get along well both personally and professionally. (L.D-WM)
- I hope to live as long as you; be as active as you are; enhance the lives of others as you do; accomplish as much as you have, and write a book about it as you are doing! (L.D-WM).

I found the following four responses too difficult to integrate, so I left them as they were sent. One is from a son who became a Catholic priest, another who became a Pentecostal Pastor. The other two are

from other sons who have progressed as professionals and are reaching out to others.

From DOMINIC FRANZ, one of my sons who became a Pentecostal Pastor. I did not integrate his response into the others. It is a bit lengthy and could dwarf the other replies.

The first thing I will use to describe You, you are an EXTRAORDINARY MOTHER, your spirituality and the love you have for God and mankind.

1. Describe me as you see me.

You are a weapon in spiritual warfare. You love prayers. You pray without ceasing.

- You are an amazing mother, full of passion to put joy on the face of those you come in touch with.
- A mother who loves and accepts her children the way God made them, bringing out the sunshine in them no matter the state of the children.
- Aunty Margaret, you are Beautiful in heart, loving, brave, caring, compassionate, cool to flow with. You are an extraordinary mother, selfless and supportive, strong and intelligent.
- You always put people before you and that's what most mothers do.

I am grateful to God for giving me a wife exactly like you!!! The verse below talks about you. Let your heart rejoice as you reflect on it because that's who you are!

I LOVE YOU
Proverbs 31:10 "Who could ever find a wife like this one—

She is a woman of strength and mighty valour!
She is full of wealth and wisdom.
The price paid for her was greater than many jewels.
....

She searches out continually to possess that which is pure and righteous.
She delights in the work of her hands.
She gives out revelation-truth to feed others.
She is like a trading ship bringing divine supplies from the merchant.
She stretches out her hands to help the needy and she lays hold of the wheels of government.
She is known by her extravagant generosity to the poor, for she always reaches out her hands to those in need.
She is not afraid of tribulation, for all her household is covered in the dual garments of righteousness and grace.
Her clothing is beautifully knit together—a purple gown of exquisite linen.
....

Even her works of righteousness she does for the benefit of her enemies.
Bold power and glorious majesty are wrapped around her as she laughs with joy over the latter days.
Her teachings are filled with wisdom and kindness as loving instruction pours from her lips.
She watches over the ways of her household and meets every need they have.
Her sons and daughters arise in one accord to extol her virtues, and her husband arises to speak of her in glowing terms.
There are many valiant and noble ones, but you have ascended above them all!"

2. What if anything attracted you to me when we first met.

I cannot say. It was a coincidence meeting you the first time that morning after Saturday morning Mass. I believe it was part of God's plan to bring me to the expected end.

Jeremiah 29:11 "For I know the thoughts that I think toward you, saith the LORD, thoughts of peace, and not of evil, to give you an expected end."
I LOVE YOU

Q. 3&4. Have I influenced your life in any way and has your life or world view changed in any way because of me and how?

Of course, yes. You have influenced my life in three ways: Body, Soul and Spirit.

You took me in the middle of a cross-road, accommodated me, clothe me, fed me and put me to school. One of the best things you wanted for all your children, especially me, was to help me get the best education in life. I am where I am because you allowed God to use you.

My spiritual life increased at the time I was with you. I can pray better now, I have the needy at heart, the passion to solve other people's challenges. Because of you I can boast that, by the special grace of God, I have put people into school, clothe, fed, and preached to them the love of God. All these will be in your account when you meet your creator. If you didn't do anything at all for mankind, I want you to remember this, you changed the life of Dominic Franz and today thousands getting into millions of people are blessed and are influenced positively because of one good deed you did by allowing God to use you. God richly bless you!!!!!

I LOVE YOU

Matthew 25: 34 " Then the King will turn to those on his right and say, You have a special place in my Father's heart. Come and experience the full inheritance of the kingdom realm that has been destined for you from before the foundation of the world! (35) For when you saw me hungry, you fed me. When you found me thirsty, you gave me something to drink. When I had no place to stay, you invited me in. (36) and when I was poorly clothed, you covered me. When I was sick, you tenderly cared for me, and when I was in prison you visited me."
(37) "Then the godly will answer him, "Lord, when did we see you hungry or thirsty and give you food and something to drink?"

Q. 5&6. What do you particularly like about me. (This is not a eulogy). And What do you particularly dislike about me - don't be afraid to say, it could help me to change for the better and I will not love you less.

I wouldn't say much here concerning what I like about you because most is said above. What I'll say is, You love God.

What I dislike about you! Ha, ha, ha, ha.

We're all a hundred percent man and a hundred percent God! Definitely we all have our weakness which is part of God's programme concerning your life. I have come to understand in the game of life that we accept people the way they are in order to influence them to improve in life.

It is very difficult to recollect what I don't like about you.
Ah, ha, I just remembered one! You stand for women against men whether they are wrong or right. You defend them. Although it's good, you over do it. Nevertheless, in all these, I still love you. I couldn't bring you millions of money, buy you houses etc. but many have been influenced through you.

I LOVE YOU

1 Corinthians 11: 1-3 "I want you to pattern your lives after me, just as I pattern mine after Christ. And I give you full credit for always keeping me in mind, as you carefully follow the substance of my instructions that I've taught you."

From ANDY SARPONG: Another adopted son who now resides in the USA

1. Describe me as you see me.

Having had the opportunity to live, grow and mature with you as a mother to me for some years, I believe my description of you will be:

- A caring, understanding person

- Someone who holds steadfast her firm faith/belief in God and is able to have a positive impact on every person with whom you come in contact
- A selfless, compassionate person who is able to put other persons first and offer any help needed regardless of the timing.

2. What if anything attracted you to me when we first met?

Honestly, for me, the objective, purpose and mission you have always embraced to date was my attraction factor. You didn't discriminate but welcomed everyone with whom you came in contact.

3. Have I influenced your life in any way?

Oh! Wow, that's a big YES. Even to the point that during my earlier years in the USA till today, you were the one person whose name I didn't and couldn't stop mentioning.

4. Has your life or world view changed in any way because of me and how?

Another big YES. Living and growing up with you offered me many blessings/opportunities that as a young teenager I couldn't fathom the extent of the changes you implanted in me.

The amazing love and care you showed me at the time when I was in most need of them have made me realize that there are still better/good people out there aiming to bring comfort, healing, and support where needed. Today, this has made me be able to offer any support, help or assistance where I can, without thinking about the payback or what I will get out of it.

5. What do you particularly like about me? (This is not a eulogy.)

Ha, ha, ha, ha! I can write a whole page if allowed, but will just make it a summary. As I have stated in the description of you and which honestly falls short of exhausting all the wonderful words that should be used to describe you, one thing I can include is that you, AUNTIE MARGARET, is a GOD send. If allowed, I will ordain you as a SAINT and ANGEL.

You are gifted with a compassionate, caring, and loving heart which leads you to interact with/accept everyone who comes your way without discrimination. One of the many things I hope to emulate in my journey through this world.

6. What do you particularly dislike about me - don't be afraid to say, it could help me to change for the better and I will not love you less.

Hmmm! Really! This is one of the toughest questions. But being my mother…the things I will consider as being my dislike of you were things that I felt as a young kid/man were necessary for me to have my way. 😊

From MAURICE AMPONSEM, another of my adopted sons

1. Describe me as you see me.

The Angel in Rough Times

2. What attracted you to me when we first met?

Our relationship with Dr. Margaret P. Price started like how the first two disciples of Jesus encountered him in John 1:35-42. nine boys, Nicholas, Edmund, James, Pascal, Sena, Dominic, Wisdom, Ebenezer and I, Maurice. Later, the number increased to twelve, and even above by the time we were all in our tertiary level. Now the story.

It was one of those Saturday mornings in the year 1995. We had closed morning Mass and, as usual, the youth of the parish met to clean the church compound. All nine boys, in our teens by then, were very active in the Catholic Youth Organization (CYO) and Knights of the Altar (Mass servers). Those days were awesome; we enjoyed being around the parish to work and play even after school. We were very eager to start a brass band group at the time, so our CYO senior crusaders gave us the task to find patrons who would help us raise funds for the instruments. After mass, we rushed to Auntie Margaret's (Dr. Margaret P. Price) car, surrounded her like soldiers just to request if she would be interested in being our patron. She said," Okay," and gave us her name. We were extremely happy, particularly listening to her accent, we knew we had hit a jackpot. It was a done deal for us, we had already received the instruments in advance. But, little did we know, that her response would lead us into a life- time friendship and relationship which would change us completely. The relationship went beyond us to our parents, other friends, and even some parishioners who all became her acquaintances. We were her joy, disciples, sons, brothers, workers. Auntie Margaret was already known by a few parishioners who were "keeping their relationship quiet" but we uncovered her. As some will say, "We blew her cover in the parish."

Now, my personal encounter with her. I gained financial support for my education and personal needs. She took interest in our education. Aside from paying our fees, which was a great relief to our parents, for me it was more like having another eye aside from my strict father. I was pushed psychologically to work extra hard in school. I attended one of the best boy's school in Ghana through her connections. Before going to Senior High School in 1998, I gained knowledge in basic computer skills as she ensured that all of us, boys, after graduating from Junior High School were enrolled in her HMC Computer Training Centre.

If anyone would recommend or commend me for being hard working and going the extra mile, I say it came from working with Auntie Margaret. I had the opportunity amongst the boys to work and travel across Ghana with Auntie Margaret after I graduated from senior high school. She made me a "workaholic" because I saw her as one who was always working extra hard and pushing for more. She never settled for less and never liked idling. Some people who knew her would flee when they saw her approaching, because she would find something for you to do. "Maurice, make sure you wake me up in 15 minutes." I would go and knock on her door and she would already be awake and ready with new ideas.

Some of us are still standing strong in our faith because we saw how faithful she was with her Christian duties, very charitable and serviceable in the house of God, a prayerful and faith driven personality. God was also faithful to her in many ways that I experienced around her. For example, contracts would come to her sometimes when she had not even submitted her bidding documents yet.

At one time, I was her driver and this was what I witnessed and have shared with others several times. Her two cars were giving her problems and she kept saying, "Maurice, I think I need a new car, and I know I am broke now." We were in Accra by then, and she said,"Let's go to Hyundai Motors show room to look at some cars." After seeing all the cars, she settled on Octavia. She requested an invoice and told them she would be back for the car. As we drove home, she made a few calls back home to her family. When the conversation ended, she said, "Maurice, my niece said she was going to send me money for the car tomorrow." To cut it short, we did pick up that car the next day.

Auntie Margaret never stopped praying. She always had her rosary in hand and would request that we pray on every journey.

I couldn't become a priest, which was my wish, because of some wrongful choices I made after graduating Senior High and even University. I remember life hitting me so hard when I got involved in a wrong relationship which led to my first marriage. I had to even flee to Liberia and stay there a while. I remember Auntie Margaret called me in Liberia and said, "Maurice, you have to come back home so we solve this problem. You know you can't hide forever." I knew that she and my Mum were always praying for me. On my return after eight months, I felt very ashamed even to go around the parish. I would hide when I went to church and tried to avoid my friends, but Auntie Margaret pushed and encouraged me. She introduced me to our new Parish Priest and told him how resourceful I was and assisted me in finding a job at the parish. I must say, that was very helpful and I really needed it. I truly became what she told the priest. I served on various parish committees and even on Parish Council as a priest nominee. Any other priest who was assigned to the parish, found me resourceful as she said. I was still battling with divorce at the time, but I was much happier then. Today, I have re-married, have stable employment and am happy.

I remember one time on our journey back from Kumasi, Auntie Margaret reprimanded me so badly that I wept in the car. It got me to quit the job she offered me without telling her and even swore not to go to her house again. But one thing I realized was you can't hide from her, she would call you. She was our mother.

In conclusion, I have come to realize maybe God brought her into my life for difficult moments and not happy or fun times. I had a great turn-around in my life because of her encouragement and her words to a priest, "Call him, he is resourceful." I remember organising the boys for us to start a foundation in her name. We were all starting some jobs around that time, therefore, couldn't contribute enough. However, I still have that dream in mind and I pray for God's will to accomplish it.

Auntie Margaret is that angel in my rough times.

From **REV. FR. HANS GERBER AGBENEFA SVD**, another of my sons.

Dr. Margaret Amoonoo-Lartson popularly known as Dr. Maggie or Auntie Margaret, I will say without a doubt, has an outstanding appearance. She possesses a good stature and could easily pass for a model. Her physical appearance is pleasing and wonderful and should you have the pleasure of meeting her, you would find it difficult to guess her age. Simply put, she is a person of great appearance. She possesses a calm, self-controlled personality, is a sweet, loving woman, and quite prim and proper when it comes to keeping rules.

The first time I set my eyes on her was at the Good Shepherd Catholic Church after Mass where she was introduced to a couple of us, the youth. I was thrilled by her sweet, melodic voice akin to an angel beckoning you to hear the Good News of God.

God has bestowed upon you, Aunt Margaret, an impressive character and a wonderful disposition. It was around the year 1996 when I first met you. I re-affirm your humility and calm demeanor. You are truly a child of God

In a very profound way, I have been influenced by you, dear Auntie Margaret, in a very positive way. No wonder you were the first to know of my admission to the seminary before I informed Fr. Andrew Campbell who recommended me to the SVD (Divine Word Missionary) Religious Congregation in Ghana.

In a more profound way, you affected, in a positive way, my life and world view. Your approach to issues and your administrative skills are indefatigable. You honestly gave me the impetus to be a missionary leaving my comfortable environment to enter the unknown in life. You assured me that God Almighty has already gone ahead of me.

Let me quickly add that just after completing Senior High School, you enrolled me, free of charge, into your firm "Health Management Consultancy and Computer School." It was a miracle because having access to the computer in those days was a luxury. There, I encountered you more often and was highly impressed with your way of doing things. Most of my friends at that time would attest to that.

I can remember how you encouraged me when I became the President of the Junior St. Vincent de Paul Society. Our many trips to the Missionaries of Charity convent was quite another experience. When I go there these days to celebrate Mass with them, I always seize the opportunity to share with them the early beginnings. Your tireless efforts and vision made that place what it is now. The memories are still fresh in my mind. God richly bless you for all these efforts. I really appreciate you.

To be concise and precise, I am really bubbling with excitement as I reflect on what I particularly like about you. I can safely say that, eulogizing you would be an understatement. You are such a wonderful person, so generous and very kind. I got my very first computer, Dell Laptop, from you as a gift for my Perpetual Vows which was to aid me in my studies albeit getting ready to finish my last year and to be ordained as a Roman Catholic priest. Without hesitation, you exhibited such a wonderful and caring character. May God truly bless you.

I really treasure you opening your home to us as boys, although you knew how troublesome we could be. You were a mother to over a hundred of us boys. My very first Christmas celebration with you was heavenly. After that first experience, we always looked forward to spending Christmas at your place, not to mention to using your swimming pool and other facilities.

I like everything about you, because what you did for me and have been for me as a mother, is awesome.

However, I used to be a bit worried about you since you trusted everyone around you and all those you encountered so easily and without counting the cost. There is one episode which I recount and which still vividly re-sounds in my ears and puts a smile on my face. This is what happened one morning at the office, which made you say, and I quote:

"Watch me. I am going to fire her," when you caught your secretary making calls and denying doing so out-rightly before us all.

You would have trusted her but, "Alas!" you caught her from the kitchen making the call.

I wish I had the time to write a lot about you. You have been a golden person. I was so proud when I had the opportunity to introduce you to the Church Congregation at Sun City on "Mother's Day."

You are really an angelic person. I always pray for you and wish you all the best in your endeavours. God bless you always, dear Auntie Margaret.

I am deeply touched by the feedback I received with regard to my legacy. It comforts me to know that my living so far has not been in vain, and encourages me to move forward in faith. It is worthy of note that I received these comments years after I had left Ghana.

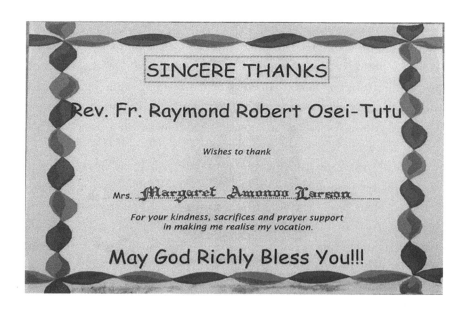

8

DEPARTURE FROM GHANA

When I decided to return to the West, I did not give much thought on how painful the actual act of departing was going to be.

Ghana had become my home, in that I now had more friends and family (adopted) there than I had in the West. Time had taken its toll and many of my friends in my age group and senior family members had passed on. However, I felt that I had made the right decision and promised to return as frequently as needed. My family in the West were glad to have me return home. One of my nieces travelled to Ghana to accompany me on the journey. I am grateful that she did.

My Niece who Came to Accompany me From Ghana
and Another son at his Ordination.

The reaction of the priests and fellow parishoners to my decision to leave made me sad. I was feasted by the parish and by the various groups to which I belonged. The following citations were presented by the Parish, the Women's Action Group on the Environment, and the St Vincent de Paul Society.

Citation from the Good Shepherd Parish

Farewell Message From Women's Action Group on the Environment

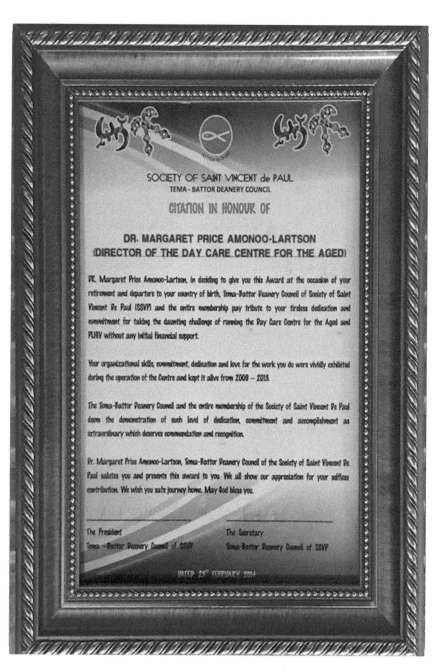

Citation From the Society of St Vincent de Paul

The Sister in Charge of the Day Care Centre Waves Goodbye

Some Children and Grandchildren

9

CONCLUSION

I thank the Lord for the gift of Service with which He has blessed me. I am definitely a work in progress. I have been richly blessed and have tried to share those blessings. Based on my observation, I believe that the feedback given by a few of my children and friends as stated in Chapter 7, is valid. I realised that most of the comments referred to my Being and not just what I had done for them materially. I am happy with the responses from some of those whose path I have crossed. I know that the majority of them are trying to follow in my footsteps. May the good Lord sustain them in their efforts to "See Christ in their neighbours."

I am comforted with the thought that I have not actually removed my hand from the plough by returning to the West. For example, while visiting with my elderly cousin who lived in a seniors' condominium in Toronto, I noted that many of the residents were not getting to Mass on a regular basis. I was able to contact the parish priest who was only too happy to arrange and say Mass with the residents on a monthly basis. When last I was in Toronto, there were as many as twenty persons at the Mass. I was also able to complete an ALPHA course a common in London, Ontario. When I am in Canada, I am still part of the Cursillo movement and the St Vincent de Paul Society.

When in Tobago, I continue my active membership with the St Vincent de Paul Society and my association with the Yahweh Foundation, whose motto is "We are our Brother's Keeper." I am still able to use the basic management and leadership skills with which God has endowed me to serve others. When I arrived in Tobago in February of 2020, my intent was to return to Canada in August of that year. However, that was not to be. COVID kept me there, and the Lord continued to use me.

I am not financially rich, I live on a small pension, but I am spiritually rich. It is why I can describe myself as a "Happy Small Islander." The house I had built for myself is still there, with my nephew as owner of the property. I myself am owner of the downstairs apartment. I had been able to return to my apartment with friends and with my husband, and enjoy my beautiful island and the rest of my family. Now that I am retired and widowed, I return every six months as a "Snow- bird." My nephew covers all utilities, including ground maintenance. He checks daily to make sure that I am "OK," that my needs are met. He takes me to the beach with him on mornings as allowed. Before COVID-19, he got me to Mass every Sunday where I was able to serve as an Extraordinary Minister. He makes sure that I get to my SVP meetings. I cannot ask for more. So, I continue to thank the Lord for His love for me, as well as for the way He protects, guards and guides me.

I know that my journey continues. I think that I have been given a break so that I could write this autobiography. Throughout my adult life, I had been trying to return to Tobago and serve the country of my birth. I had actually given up on the idea, but here I am. The good Lord, through COVID, has enabled me to finally be of some service. I was able to use my skills in helping improve the quality of service provided at the SVP Home for the Aged, which happens to be located in the village of my birth! I was also able to help with the national COVID-19 Pandemic Relief Programme. My contribution was small, I did not have to contribute materially, but of my **Being, and my time**, in helping to identify and recommend others who are in need, and in ensuring that available resources are provided through the SVP Society. To me, that is what I was told to concentrate on when I was leaving Ghana. **It was simply to continue to show love for my neighbour.**

Of all the certificates I have ever received, I feel most blessed by the one I received from His Excellencey the Most Reverend Dr. Charles Jason Gordon, the Archbishop of the Archdiocese of Port of Spain, as an expression of gratitude for services rendered to the Pandemic Relief Programme 2020.

I have revisited Ghana twice since I first left and expect to make at least one more visit. These visits enable me to attend graduations, ordinations, and weddings of my children and grandchildren. Additionally, they enable me to keep in touch with my granfather's family. I have permanent residency there and also see myself as a Ghanaian. I am forever grateful for the opportunities God gave me to serve Him there; and for the wonderful people, both secular and religious who crossed my path and drew me closer to Him. Going forward, may I be able to walk in His way wherever He takes me.

I do not know what lies ahead, but I look forward to the next chapter, because I know that the Lord is my Shepherd and He will lead me along the right path. My life is in His hands as it has always been. I pray for the grace to be able to listen to Him and do His will as I go along. In the meantime, I will continue to serve and to contribute to the activities of the SVP society to the best of my abilities.

I can definitely say that my life experiences have confirmed to me that Jesus is Lord and His love lives in my Heart. May His love be in your hearts also.

Before leaving you, I feel obliged to share with you some of what I learned along the way that helped me to overcome innumerable challenges and led to my present state of contentment, happiness, and joy. Paramount among these are:

1. Know who you are– A child of God. Don't let others define you.
2. Recognise prejudice for what it is and deal with it in a positive way. A smile confuses the enemy.
3. Always have a goal and stick to it. Always ask, "Is this or that going to help me attain my goal?"
4. Make constructive use of your sparetime, this way you won't get bored and likely to fall into temptation. "Satan finds work for idle hands."
5. Have an anchor, a focus. In my early years it was my biological mother. In my adult life, it is my spiritual mother and my Lord.
6. The act of giving back and passing on some of what the Lord has blessed you with yields more blessings than you can count.
7. Always pray for the grace of perseverance, the strengthening of your faith, humility, tolerance, love, and the ability to forgive.
8. Be considerate of others. Strive to always see Christ in your neighbour.
9. Keep the Faith. Challenges will always come, use them to strengthen you and promote your growth.
10. Patience is a real virtue. It goes along with humility. When you take things to the Lord, you have to keep an open mind and wait for the answer, which can either be, "Yes, No, or Not yet."
11. Expect pruning if you decide to give yourself to the Lord. To move from "I" to "We" from "Me" to "Us."
12. Be ever ready to learn. Admit limitations, don't be a "Know it all."

13. Involve others, they may not steal your thunder. They could make it louder.
14. Walk the talk. If as a leader you promise to do sometning, please do it. Keep your word.
15. Failure can be a basis for success; if you fall don't give up. Even Jesus fell under the weight of the cross, but he got up and gained our salvation.
16. Spiritual life is a journey of growth, not a one time event. Challenges are part of the journey. They are sent to strengthen us and deepen our faith.
17. Always strive to grow. Look for and embrace opportunities which would foster your growth.
18. The Lord speaks to us through others. Strive to learn to discern and listen to His voice.
19. It pays to have and keep a positive attitude. See the glass half full, not half empty.
20. There are Guardian Angels. They are real. Call on them daily.
21. It's never too late to fulfil your dream.
22. If you choose to serve the Lord, prepare yourself for trials. (Sirach 2:1)
23. YOU DON'T HAVE TO GIVE BIRTH TO BE A MOTHER, BE ONE. Love must be passed on. Remember: Love is not love till it's given away. It is more blessed to give than to receive.
24. Pray and give thanks always, maintain an attitude of gratitude.
25. Pray for the grace to be able to discern and do God's Will rather than your own.
26. **Stay blessed**. Always remember that God loves you. He is your Shepherd and best friend who is always ready to answer you when you call.
27. **LOVE is the answer.**

TO GOD BE THE GLORY!!!!

CPSIA information can be obtained
at www.ICGtesting.com
Printed in the USA
LVHW090707020322
712309LV00003B/75